# The Change²³

## Insights into Self-Empowerment

Jim Britt ~ Jim Lutes

*With*

Co-authors From Around the World

# The Change[23]

## Jim Britt ~ Jim Lutes

All Rights Reserved

Copyright 2025

The Change

10556 Combie Road, Suite 6205

Auburn, CA 95602

The use of any part of this publication, whether reproduced, stored in any retrieval system or transmitted in any forms or by any means, electronic or otherwise, without the prior written consent of the publisher, is an infringement of copyright law.

Jim Lutes ~ Jim Britt

The Change Volume 23

ISBN#

# Authors

Jim Britt

Jim Lutes

Tonya Drummonds

Stacy Phoenix Freeman

Sid McNairy

Renee Vee

Dr. R Harrison Baxter

Matt Orzcch

Jessa Packard

Jen Fontanilla

Halley Élise

Esther Jones-Alley

Dahlya B Shook

Bethany Stone

Ariyana Eira

Joann Marchese

Sid McNairy

Antomius Wise

Brad Balfour

Carol M. Moulton

William C. Washington

Diane A. Curran

Dr, Jackie Lau

# DEDICATION

To all those who dedicate their life to helping others live a more fulfilled life

# PREFACE

## By Jim Britt

*One of the World's top 20 life and success strategists and top 50 most influential keynote speakers*

The only constant in life is change. It swirls around us, weaving through the fabric of our existence, shaping our perspectives, molding our characters, and pushing us toward personal growth. Yet, despite its inevitability, change often comes with a veil of uncertainty and fear. How do we navigate these turbulent waters of transformation? How do we harness its power not only to survive, but to thrive?

"The Change-*Insights into self-empowerment*" is a collective journey into the heart of transformation, a treasury of wisdom from twenty-two diverse voices, each offering a unique perspective on self-empowerment. This anthology is more than a collection of essays; it is a tapestry of experiences, woven together to inspire, guide, and empower readers on their own paths of change.

As the co-creator and publisher of this anthology series, my journey began with a simple question: What does it truly mean to empower oneself in the face of change? The answers unfolded through the secrets and strategies shared by our esteemed coauthors. The depth of their insights reflects the rich tapestry of human experience, and their stories serve as both a mirror and a roadmap for those seeking self-empowerment.

The twenty-two chapters in this book are a testament to the resilience of the human spirit. Each coauthor generously shares their personal journey of transformation, offering glimpses into the moments of struggle, self-discovery and triumph. These writings are as diverse as the coauthors themselves, spanning over thirty countries, cultures, and life experiences. Yet, in their diversity, a common thread emerges—a shared commitment to embracing as a catalyst for personal empowerment.

Within these pages you'll discover several facets of the self-empowerment journey. "Awakening" is where our coauthors explore the pivotal moments that sparked their awareness and sparked their desire for change. Their stories demonstrate the transformative power of self-awareness, the first step on your own path to empowerment.

Next is "Resilience" where you can delve into the challenges our coauthors faced and the strength, they found within to overcome diversity. Whether dealing with loss, facing unexpected detours, or navigating the complexities of personal relationships, or in business, these stories illustrate the transformative nature of resilience and the inherent power within us to adapt and persevere.

Next, you'll find "Empowerment" which is the celebration of the intentional choices made by our coauthors to take charge of their lives. Through conscious decisions, mindset shifts, and a commitment to personal growth, they found the keys to unlocking their true potential. These stories and insights serve as beacons of inspiration for readers seeking to actively shape their own destinies.

And finally, "Integration" as our coauthors reflect on the ongoing journey of self-discovery and personal change. They share their practices, philosophies, and lessons that continue to guide them as they navigate the ever-changing landscape of life. These stories offer a roadmap for readers to integrate and sustain their newfound empowerment into their daily lives.

"The Change" is an invitation to explore the depths of your own potential, to embrace the certainty of change with open arms, and to recognize that within every challenge lies an opportunity for growth. It's a guide for those who seek not to just survive change but to harness its transformative power for a more empowered and fulfilling life overall.

So, as you embark on the journey through the pages of this volume of "The Change" I encourage you to approach each chapter with an open heart and curious mind, realizing that just one good idea acted upon can profoundly change your life. Let the stories and strategies shared by our coauthors be a source of inspiration, guidance, and confirmation that you too possess the power to navigate change with grace and determination and emerge stronger on the other side.

May this anthology serve as beacon of light, illuminating the path of self-empowerment and inspiring you to embrace the infinite possibilities that arise when you courageously and openly welcome change into your life.

With Gratitude and anticipation! Look forward to hearing your success story!

Jim Britt

http://JimBritt.com

# FOREWORD

## By Les Brown

Many of us spend at least a good part of our day going over internal dialog. We relive past experiences, worry about the future, blame the outside world for our shortcomings and criticize ourselves for not having all we want by this point in our lives. We do this both consciously and unconsciously. Even while we are listening to others, we aren't fully present. Instead, we are rehearsing our answers, slipping back into yesterday and worrying about tomorrow.

We live in uncertain times. We all feel we have minimum control over being able to change external circumstances, but we do have control over being able to change our internal environment, not only being able to see the truth behind a given situation but also how we respond to it. And to get the best out of the most stressful times, we need to demand the best from ourselves.

Many feel the pain of unhappiness. So many suffer from it daily, unaware that they can eliminate their suffering and find happiness by simply seeing the truth behind their unhappiness and making the right choices to change it. The problem is that our emotional conflicts are so familiar to us that they keep us blinded to better possibilities. We actually become addicted to feeling the way we do, thinking that it is just the way things are and we resign ourselves to getting by and coping.

I have had the privilege of speaking for over forty years serving millions of people from over 51 different countries. I know that there are certain patterns that create success and other patterns that breed internal conflict and failures.

The secret to being fulfilled and living the life you want is having the courage to go beyond the skills you've learned and discover the gifts that you were born with and to implement them daily. So many people settle for less in life, but I can tell you from my experience that it doesn't have to be that way.

I was born in an abandoned building on the floor with my twin brother in a poor section in Miami Florida called Liberty City. When we were six weeks of age, we were adopted by Mrs. Mimi Brown. Whenever I speak, I always say that all that I am and all I ever hope to be I owe to my mother.

When I was in the fifth grade, I was labeled educable mentally retarded and put back from the fifth grade to the fourth grade and failed again when I was in the eighth grade. Mrs. Mimi Brown took my brother and I and five other kids in as foster kids and eventually adopted us.

Because of the work that Jim Britt does and the methods and techniques he uses to change your story and how you see yourself, it enabled me to build my career to make it against all odds. Both Jim Britt and Jim Lutes are icons in personal development and empowering others to be the best they can be.

You have something special inside. You have greatness in you. When you read this book, it will take you on a journey and introduce you to a part of yourself that has remained hidden and you didn't know existed.

When you begin to look at your goals and dreams realize that you have greatness inside you. "The Change" will provide the insights and processes of self-development that will empower you to manifest your greatness.

Jim Britt and I actually started the foundation of our speaking careers in the same direct selling company, Bestline, over 40 years ago. Although I haven't followed Jim Britt's career over the years, I do know that he is recognized as one of the top thought leaders in the world, helping millions of people create prosperous lives, rewarding relationships and spiritual awareness. He has authored 15 books and multiple programs showing people how to understand their hidden abilities to do more, become more and enjoy more in every area of life.

Today, Jim Britt and mind programming expert, Jim Lutes, along with inspiring co-authors from around the world, bring a pioneering work "The Change" book series to the market to transform lives. Their principles are forged on touching millions on every continent.

As you read, you are exploring self-empowerment principles from a whole different perspective. In fact, Jim and Jim's publications of The Change book series now has hundreds of coauthors in 26 countries. The real power in each book is that 20 coauthors share their inspiring story so that the reader may benefit from their experience. It is packed with life-changing ideas, stories, tips, strategies on various empowering topics that you will love.

The principles, concepts and ideas within this book are sometimes simple, but can be profound to a person who is ready for that perfect message at the right time and is willing to take action to change. Maybe for one it's a chapter on relationships or leadership. For the next maybe it's a chapter on forgiveness or health awareness, and for another a simple life-changing message like I received as a youngster from a teacher. Each chapter is like opening a surprise empowering gift.

As I travel the world presenting my seminars, I meet people who spend more time and energy focused on what's wrong with society and their lives than is spent on helping each other improve the quality of life. With so much time spent on social media we often fear intimate contact with each other. Mistrust is often our first reaction. We judge and sometimes brutalize those among us who are in any way different from ourselves. We become addicted to anything that allows us a brief consolidation from the terrible pain we feel inside.

We need to begin to understand more about ourselves and our condition if there is ever to be the possibility of a healthy society. I believe this is possible and that's why I am so passionate about the work I do. Simply put…we are at war with ourselves. Real healing only takes place when we are willing to experience and face the truth within.

The conclusion to me is an exciting one. You, me and every other human being are shaping our brains and bodies by the thoughts we think, the emotions we feel, the intentions we hold, and the actions we take daily. Why is it exciting? Because we are in control of all these things and we can change as long as we have the intention, willingness and commitment to look inside, take charge of our lives and make the changes.

Whether you're pursuing, your dreams as an entrepreneur, a business owner or you want a more fulfilling relationship, or simply want to live a happy life, being authentic and actively appreciating what you're really capable of is going to be one of the most important assets you possess. It will make the difference between just "getting by" and really thriving and experiencing happiness or internal conflict.

Self-knowledge provides you with the emotional edge that will help you create a better life not only for yourself, but also for everyone with whom you come in contact.

This is the time to extract the best out of yourself and to use that gift to touch the lives of others.

I want to congratulate Jim Britt and Jim Lutes for making this publication series available and for allowing me to write the foreword. I honor them both and the coauthors within this book and the series for the lives they are changing.

As you enter these pages, do so slowly and with an open mind. Savor the wisdom you discover here, and then with interest and curiosity discover what rings true for you, and then take action toward the life you want.

Be prepared…because your life is about to change.

Hope to meet you one day at one of my seminars. And remember, everything you do counts!

Les Brown

# Table of Contents

**PREFACE** ................................................................. vii
**FOREWORD** ............................................................. xi
**Jim Britt** ..................................................................... 1
   Think Like Superman
**Jim Lutes** .................................................................. 13
   What You do with YOU
**Esther Jones-Alley** ................................................... 33
   I Am a Walk-In
**Jen Fontanilla** ........................................................... 43
   The AI Shift:Rewriting the Rules for Women in Creativity and Wealth
**Stacy Phoenix Freeman** ............................................ 55
   From Darkness to Light:My Journey to Freedom and Confidence
**Halley Élise** ............................................................... 63
   The Awakening of Egypt Gato. A Parable Inspired by the Sacred Alchemy of Being
**Matt Orzech** ............................................................. 75
   From Triggers to Truth:Matt Orzech's Life Transformation After Divorce
**Bethany Stone** .......................................................... 83
   The Lesson of The Lollipop
**Renee (Vee) Vardouniotis** ........................................ 93
   Think and Grow Confident
**Tonya Drummonds** ................................................. 105
   A Journey through Fear – A Destination of Freedom

**Dahlya Brown Shook** ................................................................ 113
  Going Beyond Pills & Protocols: Overcoming Dis-ease with Holistic Healthcare

**Ariyana Eira** ............................................................................ 125
  Suffering as a Conduit to Self-Knowledge and Unconditional Love

**Dr. R Harrison Baxter** ............................................................ 139
  The Mirror Within: A Journey to Empowerment through Reflective Leadership Prologue: Why This Story Matters

**Jessa Packard** ........................................................................ 149
  Some Dates Never Leave You

**Antomius Wise** ...................................................................... 163
  Intro to Life_Strategies_2.0

**Brad Balfour** .......................................................................... 173
  Finding Identity Through Memoir: Creating A Life Story Worthy for Others to Read

**Carol M. Moulton** .................................................................. 185
  My Life as a Cautionary Tale

**William C. Washington** ........................................................ 195
  Heal All Ways; Come with Motive, and Leave with Purpose

**Diane A. Curran** .................................................................... 201
  How Do You Know When You're Been Wowed?

**Dr. Jackie Lau** ....................................................................... 213
  From self-love to Self-love

**Joann Marchese** .................................................................... 225
  The Quantum Shift: Turning Pain into Power

**Afterword** ............................................................................. 235

*The Change*[23]

# Jim Britt

Jim Britt is an award-winning author of 15 best-selling books and nine #1 International best-sellers. Some of his many titles include Rings of Truth, Do This. Get Rich-For Entrepreneurs, Unleashing Your Authentic Power, The Power of Letting Go, Cracking the Rich Code and The Entrepreneur.

He is an internationally recognized business and life strategist who is highly sought after as a keynote speaker, both online and live, for all audiences.

As an entrepreneur Jim has launched 28 successful business ventures. He has served as a success strategist to over 300 corporations worldwide and was recently named as one of the world's top 50 speakers and top 20 success coaches. He was presented with the "Best of the Best" award out of the top 100 contributors of all time to the Direct Selling industry.

For over four decades Jim has presented seminars throughout the world sharing his success strategies and life enhancing realizations with over 5,000 audiences, totaling almost 2,000,000 people from all walks of life.

Early in his speaking career he was Business partners with the late Jim Rohn for eight years, where Tony Robbins worked under Jim's direction for his first few years in the speaking business.

As a performance strategist, Jim leverages his skills and experience as one of the leading experts in peak performance, entrepreneurship and personal empowerment to produce stellar results. He is pleased to work with small business entrepreneurs, and anyone seeking to remove the blocks that stop their success in any area of their life.

One of Jim's latest programs "Cracking the Rich Code" focuses on the subconscious programs influencing one's relationship with money and their financial success. www.CrackingTheRichCode.com

# Think Like Superman

## *By Jim Britt*

*"Waking up to your true greatness in life requires letting go of who you imagine yourself to be."*

--- Jim Britt

FACT: Becoming a millionaire is easier than it has ever been.

Many people have the notion that it's an impossible task to become a millionaire. Some say, "It's pure luck." Others say, "You have to be born into a rich family." For others, "You'll have to win the Lotto." And for many they say, "Your parents have to help you out a lot." That's the language of the poor.

A single mother with five children says, "I want to believe in what you're saying. However, I'm 45 years old and work long hours at two dead-end jobs. I barely earn enough to get by. What should I do?"

Another man said, "Well, if you work for the government, you cannot expect to become a millionaire. After all, you're on a fixed salary and there's little time for anything else. By the time you get home, you've got to play with the kids, eat dinner, and fall asleep watching TV."

Everyone has a story as to why they could never become a millionaire. But for every story, excuse really, there are other stories OR PEOPLE with worse circumstances, that have become rich.

The truth is that all of us can become as wealthy as we decide to be, and that's a mindset. None of us is excluded from wealth. If you have the desire to receive money, whatever the amount, you have all of the rights to do so like everyone else. There is no limit to how much you can earn for yourself. The only limitations are what you place on yourself.

Money is like the sun. It does not discriminate. It doesn't say, "I will not give light and warmth to this flower, tree, or person because I don't like them." Like the sun, money is abundantly available to all of us who truly believe that it is for us. No one is excluded.

There are, however, some major differences between rich and poor people. Here are some tips for becoming rich.

**Change Your Thinking**

You have to see the bigger picture. There are opportunities everywhere! The problem is that most people see just trees, when they should be looking at the entire forest. By doing so you will see that there are opportunities everywhere. The possibilities are endless.

You'll also have to go through plenty of <u>self-discovery</u> before you earn your first million. Knowing the truth about yourself isn't always the easiest task. Sometimes, you'll find that you are your biggest enemy—at least some days.

**Learn from Millionaires**

Most people are surrounded by what I like to call their "default friends." These friends are acquaintances that we see at the gym, school, work, local happy hour, and other places. We naturally befriend these people because we are all in the same boat financially. However, in most cases, these people aren't millionaires and cannot help you become one either. In fact, if you tell them you are going to become a millionaire, some may even tell you that it's impossible and discourage you from even trying. They'll tell you that you're living in a fantasy world and why you'll never be able to make it happen. Instead, learn from millionaires. Let go of these relationships that pull you down when it comes to your money desires. It's okay to have friends that aren't millionaires. However, only take input from those that have accomplished what you want to accomplish. Hang out with those that will encourage and help you get to the next level. Don't give your raw diamonds to a brick layer to be cut.

**Indulge in Wealth**

To become wealthy, you must learn about wealth. This means that you'll have to put yourself in situations that you've never been in before.

ON OCCASION, DO SOME OF THESE:

Fly first class and see how it makes you feel.

Eat out at the finest restaurant and don't look at the price.

Take a limo instead of a cab or Uber. Watch how you feel.

Reserve a suite in a first-class hotel.

If you are used to drinking a $20 bottle of wine, go for the $100 and see how it tastes. It does taste different.

All I am saying is, try some of the things that wealthy people do and see how it makes you feel.

## Believe it is Possible

If you believe that it is possible to become a millionaire, you can make it happen. However, if you've excluded yourself from this possibility and think and believe that it's for other people, you'll never become a millionaire.

Also, be sure to bless rich people when you can. Haters of money aren't likely to receive any of it either.

Read books that have been written by millionaires. By gaining a well-rounded education about earning large sums of money and staying inspired, you'll be able to learn the wealth secrets of the rich. I just saw a video on LinkedIn with my friend Kevin Harrington from the TV show Shark Tank. He said that one of his new companies just had a million-dollar day on Amazon.

## Enlarge Your Service

Your material wealth is the sum of your total contribution to society. Your daily mantra should be, *'How do I deliver more value to more people in less time?'* Then, you'll know that you can always increase your quality and quantity of service. Enlarging your service is also about going the extra mile. When it comes to helping others, you must give it everything you have. You just plant the seeds and nature will take care of the rest.

## Seize ALL Opportunities That Make Sense

You cannot say "No" to opportunities and expect to become a millionaire. You must seize every opportunity that has your name on it. It may just be an opportunity to connect with an influential person for no reason. Sometimes the monetary reward will not come immediately, but if you keep planting seeds, eventually you'll grow a fruitful crop. Money is the harvest of the service you provide and sometimes the connections you have. The more seeds you plant, the greater the harvest.

## Have an Unstoppable Mindset

Want to know some of what my first mentor shared with me that took me from a broke factory worker, high school dropout, to millionaire?

First, he said, you have to start thinking like a wealthy, unstoppable person. You have to have a wealth mindset. He said that wealthy people think differently. He said, "I want you to start thinking like Superman!" Sounds crazy, right? Well, it's not. It's powerful and here's why. How you think will change your life.

Wealthy people think differently. They really do. And anyone can learn to think like the wealthy.

I'm not talking about positive thinking, Law of Attraction, or motivation. Let's get real. None of that stuff works anyway. Otherwise, we would all be rich and happy already. I'm talking about thinking based in quantum physics science. Once you understand and apply it, it will change your life. You will become unstoppable!

If there was any person, fictional or real, whose qualities you could instantly possess, who would that person be? Think about it. Personally, I would say that Superman is the perfect person. Now, you are probably thinking I have lost it right? Just stick with me here. I think you will like what you are about to hear.

Superman is a fictional superhero widely considered to be one of the most famous and popular action hero and an American cultural icon. I remember watching Superman every Saturday morning when I was a kid. I couldn't get enough. He was my hero!

Let's look at Superman's traits:

Superman is indestructible.

He is a man of steel.

He can stop a locomotive in its tracks.

Bullets bounce off him.

He is faster than a speeding bullet.

No one can bring him down.

He can leap tall buildings in a single bound. Great powers to have in this day-and-age, wouldn't you say? What else would you need?

Now, for all you females, don't worry, we have not left you out. There is also a female version of Superman, named Superwoman. She has the same powers as Superman.

Now, this is where it gets interesting. Let's first look at the qualities that Superman possesses that you want to make your own. And to make it simple, I will refer to Superman for the rest of this message, and you can replace with Superwoman if you are female.

Again:

Superman is powerful and fearless.

Superman is virtually indestructible—except for kryptonite of course.

Superman can stop bullets.

Superman has supernatural powers. He can see through walls.

Superman can stop a speeding locomotive.

Superman can stop a bullet.

Superman jumps into immediate action when troubles arise.

Superman can crash through barriers.

Superman can even change clothes in a phone booth in seconds. Not too many of those around anymore. You'll have to duck behind a building to change.

So, you're thinking right now, *'Ok, I know that Superman has incredible supernatural powers, how can that help me? What good will it do me to think I am Superman, a fictional character?'*

Here is where science comes in. This is the part where you will be amazed when you learn about the supernatural powers that you already possess! NO, REALLY!

Your brain makes certain chemicals called neuropeptides. These are literally the molecules of emotion, like love, fear, joy, passion, and so on. These molecules of emotion are not only contained in your brain they actually circulate throughout your cellular structure. They send out a signal, a frequency much like a radio station sending out a signal. For example, you tune to 92.5 and you get jazz. Tune to 99.6 and you get rock. And if you are just one decimal off, you get static. The difference is that your signal goes both ways. You are a sender and a receiver.

You put out a signal, a mindset, of confidence about your financial success and people, circumstances, and opportunities show up to support your success. When you put out a signal of doubt and uncertainty and you receive support for your doubt and uncertainty. You've been around someone that you didn't trust, or you felt less than positive just being in their presence, right? You have also been around people that inspire you. That's what I'm talking about. You are projecting a frequency, looking to resonate with the frequency you are transmitting.

Anyway, the amazing part about these cells of emotion is that they are intelligent. They are thinking cells. These cells are constantly eavesdropping on the conversation that you are having with yourself. That's right. They are listening to you! And others are listening to your cells as well. Others feel what you feel when they are around you.

Your unconscious mind, your cells, are listening in, waiting to adjust your behavior based on what they hear from you, their master. So just imagine what would happen if you started to think like Superman...or like a millionaire.

Here are some of the thoughts you might have during the day:

"The challenges I face day today are easily overcome, after all I am Superman."

"I am indestructible."

"I have incredible strength."

"Nothing can stop me.....NOTHING."

"I have supernatural powers and can overcome anything."

"I can accomplish anything I want when I put my mind to it."

"I can break through any barrier."

"I can and I will do whatever it takes to accomplish my goal."

"I fear nothing."

The trillions of thinking cells in your body and brain listen, and they create exactly what you tell them to create. Their mission is to complete the picture of the you they see and hear when you talk to them. They must obey. It's their job!

Since you are Superman, you cannot fail. Why? Your thinking cells are now sending out the right signal, because you told them to. They are making you stronger, more successful, everyday! You have the ability to fight off all negativity, doubt, fear, and worry—nothing can stop you!

Superman has total confidence. So, your cells of emotion relating to confidence will now create more neuro peptide chemicals to promote feelings of power and confidence that others will feel in your presence.

Superman is fearless. So, your cells of emotion relating to fear will now create more neuro peptide chemicals to create feelings of courage. You are unstoppable!

And here's the key. Others will respond to you in the same way that you are talking to yourself.

If you are confident, others will have confidence in you.

You have thousands of thoughts every day. Make sure your thoughts are leading you in the direction you want to go. Make sure you are telling your cells a success story, and not a 'woe is me' story.

Most have been conditioned to think that creating wealth is difficult, or that it's only for the lucky few. What do you believe? It doesn't cost you any more to think like Superman; and it's much more inspiring!

Mediocrity cannot be an option if you decide to be wealthy and think like Superman.

Your decision, and communication with your cells, creates a mindset; that mindset influences how you show up.

None of that old type of thinking matters anymore…after all, you are Superman, and you can accomplish anything.

If you want wealth, you have to stretch yourself. You have to do the things that unsuccessful people are not willing to do. You have to say "yes" to opportunity, then figure out how to get the job done.

Maybe you are uncomfortable selling and asking for money. If that's the case, then learn sales and learn to ask for money every day until you feel comfortable asking for it. You will never have money if you don't learn to ask for it.

I've learned a lot in the past 40+ years as an entrepreneur. I've learned that in order to have more, you have to become more. I've also learned that if you are comfortable, you are not growing. I learned that I couldn't go from a nervous rookie speaker with minimal self-confidence to hosting TV shows and speaking in front of 5,000 people overnight. I simply wasn't ready. I grew into that, one speaking engagement at a time. Every time I finished a speaking engagement, I would ask myself, "How did I do, and how could I do it better?" I still do that today.

And I've learned from the hundreds of thousands of people I've trained, coached, and mentored that none of us can do something we don't believe is possible. It's not going to happen if you're not ready to step out of your comfort zone and stretch yourself.

This has led me to understand the single most important principle of wealth-building, that has meant the difference between poverty and riches for people since humans first traded for pelts.

Are you ready?

Come in just a little closer. Listen up!

Every income level requires a different you, a different mindset! If you think that $10,000 a month is a lot of money, then $100,000 a month will be completely out of reach. If you believe that having $5,000 in the bank would make you rich, then $50,000 won't miraculously appear. You will never earn more money than you believe is "a lot" of money.

What you do as a business is only a small part of becoming rich. In fact, there are thousands, if not tens of thousands, of ways to make money—and lots of it. What I've learned over the years is that, by focusing on who you want to become instead of what you need to do, you're going to multiply your chances of getting rich a hundredfold.

Ask anyone who's found a way to make a large sum of money legally, and he or she will tell you that it's not hard once you crack the code. And cracking the code starts with you and your mindset. The "code" to which I refer isn't a secret rite or ancient scroll. It's not even a secret. It's a certain way of thinking and believing in which you've trained your mind to see money-making ideas.

That's where you see a need in the marketplace, and you jump on the idea quickly. It might involve creating a new product; or, it may just be teaching others a special technique you've learned. It may even require raising capital to start a company or to market a product or idea on social media.

**Don't Hold Back. You Have to Take Action to Change.**

Start right now to imagine yourself as already having wealth. How would your life be? How would your day unfold? Start to own your wealth mindset now! The subconscious mind is unable to differentiate between actual fact and mere visualization. So, by imagining that you already have it, you're encouraging your subconscious mind to seek the ways and means to transform your imaginary feelings into the real thing.

Find yourself some mentors. Nobody has all the answers. Surround yourself with people that will support, inspire, and provide you with answers that keep you moving in the right direction. If you truly want to attain wealth, have a thriving business, or reach the top of your game in any endeavor, having a qualified mentor is essential.

**Okay, lets come in for a landing ...**

It is absolutely essential to have a crystal-clear picture of what you want to accomplish before you begin. If you want to attain wealth, you must learn to operate without fear and with a sharply defined mental image of the outcome you want to attain. This comes from thinking like a wealthy person, (like Superman) making decisions like a wealthy person and being fearless (like Superman) when it comes to stepping out of your comfort zone. Look at the end result as something you're already prepared to do, you just haven't done it yet.

Think about this. Your success is something that you have been preventing; it's not something you have to struggle to make happen. The key is to not let fear, doubt, other people, or mind chatter push your success away. You'll find that the solutions taking you toward your goals will come to you in the most unexpected and sudden ways. You don't need the *perfect* plan first. What you need is a perfectly clear decision about your success, the right mindset, the right mentoring, and the ideal way to get you there will materialize.

The greatest transfer of wealth in the history of the human race is happening right now. Are you positioned to get your share?

Remember, in order to get a different result, you must do something different. In order to do something different you must know something different to do. And in order to know something different, you have to first suspect that your present methods need improving.

THEN, YOU HAVE TO BE WILLING TO DO SOMETHING ABOUT IT.

***

For more information on Jim's work:

www.JimBritt.com

http://JimBrittCoaching.com

www.facebook.com/jimbrittonline

www.linkedin.com/in/jim-britt

For free audio series www.RichCode1.com and www.RichCode2.com

http://becomeAcoauthor.com

To find out how to crack the rich code and change your subconscious programming regarding your relationship with money: www.CrackingTheRichCode.com

## Jim Lutes

Say the name Jim Lutes and chances are a top performer in your company has attended one or more of his dynamic training courses over the last few years.

Having taught his branded form of human performance since the early 1990s, Mr. Lutes has accelerated top level entrepreneurs throughout his career by conducting training on personal growth and subconscious programming into worldwide markets.

During this time Jim took his skills regarding the human mind, and combining it with training on influence, persuasion and communication strategies he launched Lutes International in the early 1990s. Based in San Diego California Jim has taught seminars for, corporations, sales forces, individuals and athletes. Having appeared on television, radio and worldwide stages, Jim's style, knowledge and effectiveness provide profound results.

"Jim Lutes possesses a unique ability to create performance change in an individual in a fraction of the time it takes his competitors". The core of human decisions is based on the programs we acquire, reinforce and grow. Combining Jims various trainings individuals can reach new levels of achievement and fulfillment in all areas of life. The results are at times nothing short of astonishing.

"My goal is to take that embryonic greatness that exists inside every person in America, foster it, empower it and then hand them personal strategies based on solid principles that allow them to take that new attitude and apply it to creating a life masterpiece".

# What You do with YOU

## *By Jim Lutes*

Most people think that if they can just learn enough, earn enough, get smart enough, then they will BE enough. And they think that when that happens, they can finally relax and be happy. But what happens is that they get so caught up in what they are constantly *doing* that are not focused on how they are *being*.

In other words, they are not focused on their emotional state. When you engage your emotions, your subconscious mind begins to get the messages and begins to establish new rules and new behaviors. Then, it becomes a way of life and enters your heart and really begins to come from your heart. When it is in your heart then it is truly part of you. When you are really getting it at the deepest level, is when you can begin to anticipate what I am going to say, you know you understand it at a much deeper level right now.

I began to study human performance as a way to make some changes in my own life and when I began to see some serious results, I got so excited about it that I wanted to share it with other people. So I committed my life to learning and sharing what works with others. So, I am a committed lifetime learner and therefore I have been fortunate enough to have had the ability to look at and study just about every approach there is to personal development and success that is available in today's market. I am a strong advocate of clear, simple, workable approaches that get dependable and lasting results.

Because of the vast wealth of information my Life Masterpiece teaching gives you and the amazing results you will get, you will likely find yourself returning to it again and again throughout your life.

No matter how successful we are, or how successful we become, we all need a coach to encourage us, to challenge us, to remind us to live up to our potential. I am going to be here to do that for you each day, and it is both my honor and my privilege to serve you in that way.

Let's get started now.

The person that you are, and that person that you must become in order to put the colors of your life masterpiece where you want them and blend them in just the right combination to create your own unique experience might right now seem like two very different people, but they are one in the same. You are that person right now. I am going to help you uncover your true identity and purpose so that you can then activate the universal laws and make them work for you.

When we let go of all the stories, we have been telling ourselves about who we think we are supposed to be and what we think we are supposed to do and have, we not only free ourselves, we free our families, our children, our intimate partners, and our friends in the process. There is no way you can make a difference in yourself without touching somebody else even if it is not your intention.

The Life Masterpiece focus is about what you can do with YOU. If you want to change any circumstance, any relationship, then you must begin with yourself no matter how convinced you are that somebody else or something else must change. Changing yourself can change even the most rigid system and stubborn person. And ANY progress moves you forward. And any movement forward on your part creates the opportunity for every other part of your life to be moved forward as well.

One of the most effective ways for you to reprogram your mind is through what I like to call vicarious experiences. These are the experiences other people have had and I will bring you through their experiences by sharing their stories with you. These stories are not in this book simply to fill it up and make it fat like you find in some books. These stories are the heart and soul of the book because this is how you will begin to reprogram your subconscious and take the information into your heart where it will transform you.

The reason why vicarious experiences are so powerful is because they relate to you and so when you are reading these stories your conscious mind will get go and your unconscious mind will get the lesson.

And when you read some of these remarkable stories and meet some of these people who have gone through some amazing personal transformations, you will begin to realize that no matter who you are, no matter what part of the world you are from or what culture you grew up in, whether you grow up poor, wealthy or somewhere in between, whether you grow up with religion or Monday Night Football, you will begin to realize that we all have the same problems.

So, what will happen is you will begin to connect with these people because they have the same problems you have- the same challenges. They are universal. You will then see what the reason is for this is that we all have the same basic needs, our lives are about meeting these needs and that they impact and determine every single thing we do and every decision we make.

Every single habit, behavior, rule or pattern is your unconscious way of trying to get your needs met. And your needs are the same exact needs every other human being on the planet has. We all use different behaviors to get these needs met but they are still the same.

Some of the behaviors we use are positive and healthy and some of them are not quite so resourceful. And this is one of the reasons why, even though we all have the same needs and the same problems, we all get different results. We are hard wired with the same needs, but not with the same subconscious programming. And the reason why we all get different results boils down to one thing- standards.

You know, so often in life, we find ourselves in a position where we live life a certain way. We act a certain way. We were raised in a certain way. And through our lives in an effort to avoid pain and still meet our needs, we made critical decisions about who we are and how we think we need to be. And so we believe we know who we are.

But the way we have behaved for years is simply an *adaptation*. Something that happened in response to the desire we had to meet our basic needs- to get the love, or respect, or acceptance from a parent, lover, loved one or peers- caused us to make a key decision and adapt to the circumstances around us. We do not ever realize that for years we have been living something that we are really good at but which is not necessarily our true nature.

One of the things you will learn here is that a single decision has the power to change everything in a heartbeat. In fact, when you stay with me through this you are going to learn about a decision, I made perhaps some time ago that determines the choices you have made in the course of your life up until now. Today he made a decision to pick up this book and begin this journey with me and if you will indulge me for just a few hours the decision to pick up this book might be the decision that changes everything in your life from today on.

Now that you've made the decision to read it, I will tell you what this book can really do for you. It will get you to uncover and maybe for the first time really identify how the role models of your life have affected your subconscious decision-making in ways you never dreamed possible.

Without getting into the actual science behind it, a child's brain works much differently than an adult brain. As you might already know our brains operate using four different wavelengths -- alpha, beta, theta and delta. Most of the time, the adult brain operates at the beta level when we are awake. The beta level is when our eyes are focused in our conscious mind is in control, and we are logical. The alpha level is a level that we must pass through to go to sleep and to wake up, and it's also the most common level is one we are in a trance. Theta is for a deeper trance or dreaming, and delta is for deep sleep.

This means that when we are at the alpha level, we are highly impressionable, because the messages are going directly into our subconscious minds. A child's mind is different because it operates primarily at the alpha level, which is why children are so impressionable. This also means that our parents and other significant people in our childhood had a tremendous impact on the messages that are subconscious mind received and events from our childhood had a strong impact on our self-image, our identity and how we develop as adults. This is why when we speak about reprogramming the subconscious mind is very important to talk about her childhood and her relationship with her parents. This is not done to point fingers or place blame, but to help us understand some of the reasons for the choices that we make for the patterns that we keep repeating and how they carry over from generation to generation.

Even if you feel like you held your own when you were growing up, and that the relationships that you had as a child -- especially the relationship she had with your mother and father -- were strong, and you feel like you are strong as a result. There are still patterns that your subconscious mind is running that no longer serve you. Because it's the tension, the experience of having to deal with all of the events of your past and even the events that happened before you were born in your parent's past -- all of these experiences affect your decision making, your relationships, your finances, your choices, behaviors and life circumstances, even today.

Even if your childhood was perfect and you feel like you honor, respect and love your parents and adore all of your siblings and even if your parents or your greatest role models, you are still affected on many levels and in many ways. And because you decided to read this book, I believe you have some things you would like to change. If you change anything, first you must learn to reprogram your subconscious mind and part of doing so is to understand that the key decisions you made in the past still impact you today.

Our childhood role models deeply affect both our conscious and subconscious decision-making and behavior patterns. We are all examples, and some of us are warnings. We all, at one time or another, impact other people. This is one of the reasons why I stress that it is so important to live consciously and be an example.

When I ask people about their belief systems and the habits and patterns that basically control their lives, I am often struck by how few of these beliefs and habits were ever chosen by that person on a conscious level. In other words, the rules that are guiding your life about how to BE in your own life very often picked up unconsciously.

It is incredible how common it is that people start this process, and when they begin to reassess their lives and their relationships with themselves and others in the success they are having or perhaps not having, they discover that much of what has been screwing up their lives, their achievements, their finances, their careers, their intimate relationships, and even their bodies (and I am not talking about the excuse many of us use about genetics. Being the reason, our bodies look the way they do) was influenced by their PARENTS. Not by their parents' problems, but by somehow trying to be liked, loved or appreciated by one parent. Many times, these decisions also have to do with trying to avoid pain that was inflicted by a parent or other significant role model, or simply standing up to a parent.

We can be 40, 50 or even 80 years old, and we are still living the strategies of a child.

And what's even worse, is it very often when we were a kid, we said, "I'll never be like that!" And here you are today, exactly like that! You don't want to admit it but if you held up a mirror and watched a film of your interactions you would say, "Oh my God, I never wanted to be like that parent." And yet you are. Or perhaps you have done the opposite. Perhaps you have thrown the pendulum the other way and you're not like that parent at all. Now, you are something worse. Or, let's just say you are something else. You are the opposite of the extreme you didn't like. And so now you are another extreme, that doesn't work either. Because no one teaches us this stuff, and so it becomes unconscious. We don't even see it. It's part of the invisible fabric of our thinking and our decision-making every single day.

This book will give you a unique opportunity to look deep inside yourself. It will allow you to look inside of your relationships, your decisions about money, and your decisions about your career, your relationship with God or your higher power, and even your body. It will allow you to understand how your own upbringing us may be influenced you and you probably know a lot of the ways it has influenced you, but maybe you'll spot some of the decisions you have made, maybe even one core decision that has affected your identity.

So, what the heck does identity mean anyway? It can be such a big and often loaded word. Well, I believe identity is the strongest force in human personality. If you want to know what shapes you the most it's not your capability. It's your identity and the rules you have for who you think you are.

And you know what the challenge is? Most of us defined ourselves a long time ago. And when we step outside that definition, we get uncomfortable, because the strongest force in the human personality is the need to remain consistent with how we define ourselves. Later,

## The Change

we will talk about the human needs referred to earlier. One of them is certainty. What this means is that if certainty is one of the deepest needs we have, then if you don't know who you are, you do not know how to act.

Very early in life, we begin to define who we are. We use labels such as loner, aggressive conservative, sexy, successful, loser, rich or poor.

I work for others. I am ugly. I am smart. I am a procrastinator. I am clumsy. I am athletic. I am thin. I am big boned. What happens is these definitions become self-fulfilling prophecies because nobody wants to be disappointed. Nobody wants to live in a place of uncertainty. So, there may be arranging your identity or in your definition of yourself, but it may not be absolute.

The metaphor that you so often hear what we talk about our comfort zone, is that our comfort zone is like a thermostat. We all have our comfort zone, and it is set by our subconscious mind. So, if your subconscious mind has set your thermostat in a particular area of your life, for example how much money you make, that let's say 45°, and if the temperature drops down to 40°, guess what happens? It doesn't meet your identity. In other words, things are not good enough, whether it be mentally and emotionally financially with your weight (which by the way is the primary reason people whose weight tend to gain it back because they lose it before reprogramming their subconscious mind to reset the thermostat) or whatever.

For example, if you drop down to 40° and your finances and 45° is your identity. This means that 45° is what you must have. Or, if you drop down to 70° in your intimacy and 80° is your identity, then this is what you must have. Whatever it is, when you drop below your comfort zone, you will be compelled to drive to make it better automatically. If your body gets out of control, there is a point at which you go, "that's enough!" You are willing to be a little off your identity but not that much. And suddenly you go on the diet suddenly make the change because you feel the pressure that comes with being inconsistent with your own definition of how you think you should be.

But what most of us fail to recognize is that this happens on the other side as well. Your subconscious mind since your mental thermostat at say 45° for your finances or 80° mentally for how close you want to be with your intimate partner, or 70° for how your body should look and feel,

This is not your *goal*. Your goal is something much larger. This is your subconscious comfort zone or your subconscious definition of yourself. For example, you might think of yourself as big boned, but if it suddenly isn't good enough and you really become overweight, then you change to fit your self-image or your definition of yourself in order to get back into that comfort zone. But also, if it gets better than you expected, perhaps, you lose a lot of weight and get really good shape, or perhaps you lead your company in sales for two quarters in a row when you normally come in third or fourth, or perhaps you jump from 70° in your intimacy, and now you have a relationship that is at 90 or even 100°. You have a really hot, passionate relationship with more passion than you ever have before, or you lose three dress sizes instead of one, or you double your income, whatever it is, your subconscious mind starts talking some sense into you. And your brain goes, "Hello, dude what the heck are you doing? You are 70 degree-er, what in heck are you doing way appear at 90? You can't keep that. That's not gonna last. Get back down to 70° before you get hurt or fail or screw it up. You're in over your head. You're not an entrepreneur. You work for other people."

Wherever your subconscious mind has set your comfort zone based on the way you define yourself, you're going to keep adjusting to stay in that comfort zone. So many times, in these types of programs, people challenge you to get out of your comfort zone, which you can't do consciously. You have to go into your subconscious and reset your comfort zone, just like you would the thermostat. And this will keep happening until you reprogram your subconscious mind with a new identity, and the new comfort zone. Before you set out to make any kind of lasting change, you must reset your subconscious comfort zone.

And what do we do when we exceed our comfort zone? Well, what happened is that the drive to make things better stops. And so you stop growing and gradually you drift back until you reach your comfort zone. Or worse, you start to sabotage. The mental air conditioners kick on and bring yourself right back down to where you think you deserve to be based on your subconscious identity.

For example, if the only kind of love you view as a child was abuse, the only kind of life. You knew was living paycheck to paycheck or in debt, or the only kind of lifestyle you ever experienced with sedentary, whatever it is, even though it might be painful. It is what you know. This becomes your comfort zone and therefore provides the certainty that you need. It becomes your self-definition and what you think you deserve. You begin to think -- not consciously, but unconsciously -- this IS love, this is just the body. You inherited, or that wealth is for other kinds of people, or you're not the right kind of person to make certain kinds of social contacts. Of course, this is not your conscious thinking that this is what is going on in your subconscious.

And therein lays the trouble, or perhaps a better way to say it, the shortcomings with many of the programs you may have tried in the past. They pump you up and felt good about it. They motivated you with affirmations and taught you to use visualization. They've even taught you that the universal laws work for everyone. You may have even made some changes, but they did not last. Because when you're taught these things, you know the stuff in your head on a conscious level. But your identity and self-definition is the thermostat of subconscious mind, so before you can make any substantive or lasting change, first you must reprogram your subconscious mind and change who you are at the deepest level. (Green papers).

In other words, you must become the kind of person who has whatever it is that you want. Visualizing it, affirming it, and even living your life by a new set of standards is not going to work long term until this stuff goes from your conscious to your unconscious and finally into your heart. Not only do you have to DO it, and not only do you have to LIVE it, but you also have to BECOME it. And then you will manifest it.

And that is the difference between the stick figure you are drawing now or the paint by numbers life you have been taught to lead and the masterpiece you are now creating. So, for the colors in our masterpiece is to really live consciously, to be an example, then we have to get conscious about what is shaping us and the thing that shapes you most identity.

Someone who is outrageous will behave, say things differently and move differently than someone who believes they are extremely conservative. They will use a different voice, a different way of moving and a different language. Here is my question for you:

When did you come up with this definition?

When did you decide who you are?

When was the last time you updated it?

Maybe it's time to take another look at who you are today. And maybe you don't have to actually give up your identity. Maybe the identity created for yourself is magnificent, but maybe it's time to expand it. Maybe it's time to add to it. Maybe it's time to open up to a new level of freedom and options.

And when you do that there will be a processional effect in all areas of your life, because we are all connected in a cybernetic loop. If I want to change you, I can try to control you, but that will not change anything. Or I can try to change the system, but that will not last or will be futile. Or I can change me into an ID so that everything changes.

For example, if I change the way I treat you, the way I respond to you, my voice my body my feelings and my emotions by respect for you. It will affect the way you feel and the way you respond back. And the same is true with the universe and higher intelligence. Once you change yourself, reprogram your subconscious, become the person you need to become that the things that you want in your life, then you will begin to receive a different response from the universe in a different result in your life. Then begin to experience your life as a masterpiece.

You will learn that what we value controls what we are willing to do or not do -- in our businesses, and our relationships, with our bodies and with our children. Some people get locked in place into a mindset. I call it being committed to your commitment. For example, have you ever been in an argument, and you were so angry that as the argument progressed, you forgot what you were angry about, and it just became about winning? We've all been there and what happens is we get committed to being angry and said that resolving the argument. Or we get committed to being right, instead of uncovering the truth. When this happens, get so wrapped up in our commitment that we can no longer see the forest through the trees. We lose touch with what we really want, because we get stuck in a mindset, and we get committed to our commitments.

(Judy- discovers a decision she made as a child and uses the discovery to transform her life and her children and grandchildren's lives).


Today, you are beginning a process that can truly change the quality of your life forever and can take that paint by numbers life you might be living now and create the masterpiece called your life. So just for a moment now, what I want you to do is imagine that your life is a painting. And imagine that you have died and are looking down at that painting. What did you leave behind? Is your life, a masterpiece that is cherished and hangs prominently as an example for others of what is possible, or is it a paint-by-numbers life that is packed away in someone's basement?

As you begin this process, I asked for only two things from you:

- Your heartfelt desire to make real changes.
- The commitment to follow through and do this, as simple or as located as it might seem in the moment.

If you can do just those two things, then the things that you used to call dreams will become part of your daily reality.

Why is it that you can have a person who seems to have superior abilities, talents, skills, and education, at the same time, they don't produce the quality of life they want or that you might expect from them? And why is it, on the other hand, you can have someone who seemingly has every disadvantage -- no family support, the wrong social status, no emotional support, no education, and the wrong background -- and yet they go out and produce results, way beyond what anyone could have expected or even imagined?

The difference in our quality of life is not about our capability, background or education. Human beings, *that means you*, are *all capable* of achieving incredible results, and yet sadly only a few seem to get it.

What people WILL do is very different from what people CAN do.

I want to challenge you right now to start using your WILL muscle, instead of your TRY muscle, which is probably overdeveloped anyhow. I challenge you to start exercising your inborn human power, which is your birthright as a member of the human race, your ability to act based on the choice and free will that every human has in equal measure. Frankly, this means that if it has been achieved, then there is no reason on earth why you cannot achieve it. And beyond that, if it can be imagined, then there is also very little reason why you cannot achieve it. As a matter of fact, your unconscious mind will rarely imagine something that you are capable of. That is the difference between desires and fantasies. It's true. There are no excuses anymore. If you are reading this and you are a human being that you have the ability to take action and to produce results.

The disability that I'm talking about is not something I can give you. Why? Because you already have it. You were born, great. Now, I challenge you to go out and take back what is rightfully yours.

Hopefully, something is now a weekend within you in two ways. One, by igniting your desire and two by showing you some simple systematic strategies on how you can get greater results on a daily basis.

When most of us think of success or failure, we tend to think of these monumental things. Failure is not an overnight thing, and neither is success.

Just what is success? Well, some people describe it in terms of achievements like a resume. But it is different for everyone. So, some people describe it as a feeling.

The truth is that success is wrapped up in failure. What I mean by that is that success is simply a string of failures all going in the same purposeful direction. That's right. If you want to find success you have to look inside a failure. In other words, if you want to be more successful than the next person, then you simply have to be willing to experience more failure, but not just any failures. You must be willing to take specific actions, based on specific decisions, that may fail most of the time, but keep going, perhaps with a new strategy, experience and more failures, and eventually you will succeed. If this sounds painful, then I want you to think for a moment about what true failure actually is.

True failure is lifelong failure. It is the failure of inactivity. It's not actually failing at what you DO -- those things will lead to success. But when you fail to DO, you fail to succeed. In failing to do is a recipe for ultimate failure in life. When you fail to make the calls, when you fail to follow through, when you fail to say I love you, when you fail to give your all, that is what creates the ultimate failure in life. Ultimate failure creates the greatest pain, the feelings we want to avoid at all costs. Now *that* is painful.

Success happens one step at a time. Success happens one failure at a time. It is successfully making the calls and doing it no matter how long it takes for the outcome in the moment. It is successfully getting up and following through. It is successfully making sure that you make that unique contact. It is successfully breaking through the limits that used to stop you.

Success is a combination of all those little things -- those little successes that often come disguised as failures -- over each day and over your lifetime that eventually create a life that you will have total pride and great joy in knowing that you created your life and made it into a masterpiece of your very own -- a life that is an example to others as how it is done.

The purpose of Life Masterpiece is to show you how to tap the power you were born with and how to tap into it every single day. And to make it an effortless process so that it becomes a lifestyle.

Before I go any further, I want to thank you for your friendship. Even though I have never met you, personally, I feel as if you and I are kindred spirits. The reason why say that is it you picked up this book. You made an investment. You're now reading it. This means you are one of the few who will do what others will not. This puts you light years ahead of 99% of the people. You and I encounter every day. Those people are living a paint-by-numbers life. They want to change, but they just do not get it, because they haven't got the first clue what they want and worse, they are not willing to do anything to change it.

I know you're special because you are researching and exploring and because you are reading this. It says something to me about you. It tells me that you are willing to do what it takes to succeed. It tells me that you are not satisfied with your life, and you will not be satisfied until you have successfully created your own masterpiece. So, I really want to give you the tools that can make a difference.

I have dedicated my life to understanding what makes people do what they do. What drives you? What is it that makes the difference in performance from one human being to the next? If we are all born with the same stuff, what causes some to tap into it and others to settle for a mediocre, paint-by-numbers existence?

Power comes from concentrating your focus and taking daily action to improve something. Even a 1% improvement today can result in unbelievable change, because 1% per day will not give you a 365% difference in being the year, because it builds and compounds to create a difference, way beyond anything you can probably imagine right now.

I will show you how to make it happen quickly, not 10 or 20 years from now, but today. Anything you commit to and focus on everyday must improve.

The challenge is that most of us do not know WHO we are, and therefore do not know how to control our mental focus. In fact, most of us focus on what is not working and spent most of her energy focusing on what we DON'T want by asking questions like, "how come this always happens to me?" If you focus on that enough, then that is what you will continue to experience. (Universal laws don't work unless you reprogram).

I am going to show you how to refocus your mental energy and reprogram your subconscious, so that you can ask better questions and therefore get a better result. Whatever you focus on, you manifest, which is why the Law of attraction won't work until you know what you want at the deepest level of your mind.

The key is to get you to live by those factors. Most people focus on the small stuff. I know you are to believe this, or you would not have picked up this book. Most people are so focused on what they have to DO. In other words, they focus on their to-do list, how to make a living instead of how to create their life. You could so easily get caught up in the day-to-day experiences that you tend to make a monument of the port in your mind, when actually in the long term these things that seem monumentally important now are actually quite trivial.

To create your masterpiece, you have to learn how to take care of the big things -- each color in your crayon box -- mentally, emotionally, physically, financially, and spiritually. Here are two things that usually lead to ultimate success -- either inspiration or desperation. Desperation can be a good thing because until you get really dissatisfied. You won't do anything to take your life to another level. Dissatisfaction is awesome! If you are completely satisfied, you will get comfortable. They may life begins to deteriorate.

My guess is that you invested in this book because on some level you are dissatisfied.

("If you make enough money, at least you can handle your problems in style" R)

(Lots of money, beyond comfort zone)

"It's a funny thing, the more I practice the luckier I get" AP

Subconsciously, most of us have an idea of what we think we deserve. This is our comfort zone, in which the subconscious mind determines when it sets our internal thermostat. Your subconscious mind has set your internal thermostat, and so when you begin to achieve, perhaps make a lot of money, you begin to sabotage your success dropping down to where you subconsciously think you deserve to be.

The past does not equal the future. Even if you are jaded and cynical, you've tried everything, this moment is a great new opportunity if you've tried other programs in the past that nothing has really changed your lifelong term. I believe that all it has done is it has prepared you for this program. And at some level if you did not believe that, then you would not be reading this right now.

Life Masterpiece is very different from other programs you may have tried. You will not find affirmations and visualizations and motivations in this book. What you will find is the answer to what is keeping you back, and how to reprogram your subconscious mind and how to use it to create.

Your brain is the most powerful computer on the planet. When you learn to use it properly, you can create any result you want. And they can give you the answer to almost any problem you have. The problem is that this computer, we call our brain, is not user-friendly, and does not come with an owner's manual. Life Masterpiece will show you how to operate your supercomputer with precision. Lasting change is not created in your life by learning more. Lasting change is created by using your own power to take action.

We're going to recondition the way your mind works by reprogramming your subconscious. This will change the way you feel and the way you behave for the rest of your life. Just as there have been extraordinary technological, scientific, and medical breakthroughs in the past two decades there has also been a breakthrough in the science of quantum physics. While we are not going to learn specifically about quantum physics in this book, we are going to take and use part of that technology. Because the latest cutting-edge tools for creating lasting change come from breakthroughs in quantum physics that have to do with human technology and how to get new results in record time.

There are four steps to success:

1. Know what you want. It is important for you to know what you want, and for you to know how you want things to turn out. In other words, you must know your outcome before you begin. The first step is to decide what you want out of whatever situation you are currently in. The clearer you aren't what you want, the more you will empower your brain to give you the answers.

2. You must use it. In other words, you must get yourself to take action toward your outcome. This means that you must put energy in the right direction, even when you do not know exactly what to do. Many people do not know what to do first. I will teach you exactly what to do. Some

people want to know what happens if they try, and it doesn't work. I can tell you right now, and you will learn why in this book, why nothing you try will ever work. So how do you take action? Decide to. It's not about what you can do. It's about what you will do.

3. Notice your results. It's not enough to take action. You must also pay attention to the results you are getting from your actions. Do your actions always work? No. Remember, success is just a series of failures, but failures with the purpose, failures directed at a specific result. You know what you want; you took action, now notice the result. (JS-obstacles and timing).

4. Be flexible and willing to change your approach. You must be willing to make changes and adjustments based on the results of your actions, because flexibility is the key to the system. In other words, if you notice that what you are doing is not working. And you're not getting closer to your goal or even getting further away, instead of feeling like a failure in giving up. Sometimes you simply need to change your approach.

There is a way to speed this up. Instead of just knowing what you want, taking random actions, I will show you a way to increase the pace and the certainty of your success.

("Knowledge is not power. Knowledge is potential power." R)

You may be thinking, "Jim, if this is a simple, how come everyone isn't doing it?" The answer is because the majority of people tend to get caught up in the day-to-day trivialities such as paying their bills. Now, paying your bills might seem monumentally important to you, but honestly, can you think of anyone who has ever reported that they were successful in life because they mastered the art of bill paying? I am not saying that you shouldn't pay your bills, what I'm saying is that you should know I yourself to get caught up in something trivial and make it something big, so that you can use it as an excuse for not doing the really important things in life. At the end of your life, no one is going to remember whether or not you paid all of your bills and what a wonderful job you did of it. In other words, people get caught up in making a living instead of creating a life. They come to the end of their life dissatisfied because they realize they only live 10% of it, not because they were not capable or intelligent, and not for a lack of knowledge, but simply because they never had a clear idea about what they wanted.

Some people think that what they really want is a program that deals with only one area of your life like that business program. If that is what you are thinking, let me tell you right now that Life Masterpiece is one of the most powerful business programs because it deals with the source of all your business -- YOU. When you are better will be a better speaker, salesperson negotiator. Your creativity will flow freely. Mobile to manage and influence people far more effectively than you can now. The first step to changing your career and your business is to change yourself.

***

To contact Jim:

www.lutesinternational.com

info@lutesinternational.com

https://www.facebook.com/jimlutes

https://mindmotionacademy.com

# Esther Jones-Alley

Esther Jones-Alley is a Spiritual Architect and Conscious Living Coach who helps leaders, visionaries, and seekers unlock their potential and achieve deep fulfillment. Through her signature "Soul Evolution Matrix," she blends intuition, empathy, and practical strategies to guide clients toward profound personal and spiritual transformation. Known for her compassionate and empowering style, Esther supports individuals in designing an authentic, joy-filled life.

Her journey from external success to true fulfillment fuels her unwavering dedication to personal growth, conscious leadership, and spiritual awakening. With over 25 years of executive-level experience in program and project management—spanning politics, local government, nonprofit leadership, and entrepreneurship—she has honed her expertise in coaching executives, corporate leaders, employees, and families through transitions. Her work focuses on career alignment, job dissatisfaction, major life changes, family dynamics, healing childhood trauma, conscious relationships, and spiritual awakening.

Esther is an ordained interfaith/inter-spiritual and metaphysical minister and a Professional Certified Life Coach through the International Coaching Federation (ICF). She is the author of *The Centered Life: A Spiritual Life Coaching Journey* and a contributing author in *Limitless* (July 2023). As a sought-after international speaker, she shares insights on transformation, intuitive wisdom, and personal evolution.

Committed to lifelong learning and deepening her ability to serve, Esther is currently pursuing a Doctorate in Metaphysical Sciences. Her work is a bridge between practical transformation and spiritual awakening, helping others reconnect with their truth and step into their highest calling.

# I Am a Walk-In

## *By Esther Jones-Alley*

I had broken free. Free from expectations, free from the constraints of my upbringing, and free to explore a world that felt entirely my own. My sister and I were living life as if it were golden, embracing a lifestyle that couldn't have been further from the one we had been raised in.

We lived fast. Hard. Reckless.

Drugs were never out of reach—we had whatever we wanted whenever we wanted it. Mornings started with a joint, weekends were fueled by a chaotic mix of uppers and downers, and the freezer always held a few coke hits for when we needed an extra kick. A shoebox stuffed with weed sat in the cabinet like an afterthought. We worked hard all week, but our real lives began the moment Friday rolled around.

I was twenty-three, a single mother to my three-year-old daughter, Ieshia. My sister, Ruth, child-free by choice, had no interest in slowing down. Together, we had escaped our small-town roots and the weight of our profoundly religious family, trading it all for the bright lights and boundless possibilities of Long Beach.

Ruth worked at a fish cannery in San Pedro, while I put in my hours at a lamp factory in Long Beach. The pay wasn't much, but it was enough to keep us going—to fuel the weekends, the indulgences. I took pride in my collection of high-heeled shoes and my bright yellow Volkswagen Bug, custom-fitted with a Rolls-Royce front end. That car was my signature. Its four-speed transmission kept me sharp on nights when the drugs had drained me, forcing my mind to stay alert.

"Living for the weekend." That was our motto.

Our circle included Hattie, my running partner, who had three kids of her own. But with family nearby, she always had a built-in babysitter, giving her the freedom to run the streets with us. Our nights belonged to the hottest clubs in LA, where the party never really stopped. When the bars shut down at 2 a.m., we moved to after-hours spots that pulsed with music until dawn. By the time we left those, the sun would already be creeping over the horizon, and we'd head to Denny's or I-Hop for breakfast before finally dragging ourselves home mid-morning.

We had strayed far—so far—from the strict religious teachings of our childhood. But at the time, we didn't care.

We were free.

Or so we thought.

## A Warning

Five or six months before everything changed, our mother sent word that our bishop wanted to speak with us about our lifestyle. We went to church as requested, expecting another sermon, perhaps a gentle rebuke, but nothing life changing.

After the service, we met with the bishop, hoping for some uplifting prophecy. Instead, the moment I sat down, he gasped, his face paling as if he had seen something beyond the physical.

"You just took her place," he whispered.

I didn't understand what he meant. Not then. But I would soon find out.

The bishop, usually soft-spoken and given to parables, was uncharacteristically direct that day. He warned us to change our ways, his voice weighed with urgency. *"If you don't, you will perish."*

Then he told us about a vision he had—a spiritual warning. In it, he had tried to reach my sister and me, desperate to save us. But before he could, a lamb stepped in his path, blocking him from moving forward. He had tried to go around it, but the lamb would not let him pass.

*"Return to the church,"* he pleaded with us. *"Slow down before it's too late."*

We nodded. We said we would.

But we didn't.

## A Brush with Death

Not long after the bishop's warning, I fell ill. Initially, I dismissed it, believing I had just partied too much. However, as the days dragged on, I realized this was different. Something inside me was failing.

I took several desperate trips to the emergency room, but the doctors found nothing. Meanwhile, my body wasted away. My clothes hung loosely over my thinning frame, my bones pressing against my skin like fragile twigs. The reflection in the mirror became unrecognizable. Fear settled deep within me.

Weeks passed in a blur of exhaustion and pain, but I forced myself back to work, clinging to routine as if it could anchor me. The moment my supervisor saw me, she paled.

*"You need to see a doctor. Now."*

When I finally received a diagnosis—hepatitis—there was no relief, only a quiet, sinking acceptance. Another girl from my town had recently died from it, and I knew my fate was sealed.

The doctor spoke of rest, a bland diet, and time to heal. But in my heart, I knew—I was dying.

That night, as I lay in bed, the room closed in around me with a suffocating stillness, and a voice called my name.

Clear. Loud. Unmistakable.

My eyes flew open. My breath caught. I sat up, scanning the room, but I was all alone.

Yet I *felt* something there.

I knew, in that chilling moment, that Death had come.

## Realization and Transformation

Fearing the end, I moved through my days with quiet resignation, visiting family and old friends, making sure my affairs were in order. When I stopped by my mother's house, I confronted my younger sister about her reliance on our mother's generosity. As expected, my mother leapt to her defense.

Her eyes flashed with anger, and she raised her hand to strike me—but then, she froze. Her face drained of color, her entire body trembling. Instead of anger, I saw something else take over her expression—fear.

She burst into tears.

"All I saw was blood when I went to hit you," she sobbed. "You are dying."

There was nothing left to say. I had already made peace with my fate. I returned to my Long Beach apartment, waiting for what felt inevitable.

But before the week was out, one of my brothers arrived, urgency in his voice. *"Mom and Bishop want you home immediately."* I was too weak to argue. Days later, my brothers came to pack my things, bringing me back to the place where I had once felt safe.

At my mother's house, time blurred. I spent most of my days asleep, yet sleep was unlike anything I had known before. Every time I closed my eyes, I was met with an endless, bright white nothingness—pure, vast, and strangely peaceful. I'd never felt so good in all my life.

Then, one day, my oldest brother rushed into the room, his face streaked with tears.

*"You have to go to the hospital. Bishop sent me. He said she's dying."*

The doctors confirmed it.

*"If you know how to pray,"* one of them told my mother, *"you better start. There's nothing more we can do. It's in God's hands now."*

I was placed in quarantine for fourteen days, drifting in and out of awareness. Each day, my mother woke me—feeding me, bathing me, and, most importantly, praying by my side.

But the nights... the nights were something else entirely.

Every time I slept, I was transported into vivid, intricate dreams—a life review unfolding before me. I relived moments from my childhood with startling clarity, not as a passive observer, but as if I were *there* again, fully immersed.

Each morning, when my mother came to my bedside, I bombarded her with questions about things I *shouldn't* have remembered—events from when I was just a baby, illnesses I had suffered, details long buried in the past. She confirmed every single one of them.

Still, my body did not heal. The doctors, desperate for answers, scheduled a liver biopsy. The news filled me with dread. I *knew* I couldn't endure it. I *knew* I didn't want that procedure.

Then—something changed.

## The Night I Didn't Dream

As I prepared for sleep that night, I hummed a hymn—one I can no longer remember. The melody drifted from my lips like a whisper to the universe, carrying with it a quiet surrender. A deep sense of peace swept over me, lifting something unseen from my spirit.

And then—nothing.

It was the first night I didn't dream. The first night, I remember absolutely nothing. A complete void, as if time itself had paused.

The next morning, the warmth of the sun stirred me awake. Golden, vibrant light poured through the window. I sprang from my bed, drawn to it, my heart pounding with an unusual exhilaration. As I gazed outside, everything felt fresh. I had never seen the sun before, yet I understood what it was on an intellectual level. I glanced down and saw the trees and grass, feeling similarly; I understood what they were intellectually but had never seen them before.

And I knew, beyond a shadow of a doubt, that I didn't belong there.

When the phlebotomist arrived to draw my blood, I told him, *I'm going home today.* He chuckled, dismissing my words. But I knew. My mother was equally skeptical when I called her, insisting she'd visit as usual, certain I wouldn't be discharged.

Yet, when the doctor finally entered my room, I was restless and determined. The urgency within me was unshakable. He spent half an hour trying to calm me and reasoning with me until he finally sighed and said, *"Let's make a deal."*

"If you gain five pounds and your bile count improves, you can go home."

By the following day, my test results had left him speechless. My bile count had returned to normal, and somehow—I had gained five pounds overnight.

"I've never seen anything like this," he admitted, shaking his head. "Not in all my years as a doctor."

And just like that, I was discharged.

But the real mystery wasn't in the test results. It wasn't in the numbers or the weight I had gained. The real mystery lay in the night before—the night that was missing from my memory.

The night I didn't dream.

## The Awakening: A Journey Beyond the Known

When I returned home, people kept telling me how different I looked. They noticed it in my eyes since the color had changed slightly, and in how I carried myself—there was a sense of peace about me that hadn't existed before. But what they couldn't see was that I had been given more than just a second chance at life. I had been given a doorway to something far more significant—a purpose I had yet to comprehend.

A deep hunger for knowledge consumed me. I devoured everything I could find on spirituality, the universe, and the intricate web that connects us to the divine. I explored all the major religions, hoping for answers, but none could explain what had happened to me. I wasn't just searching for understanding—I was searching for *myself.*

Yet, the strangest part of my transformation wasn't just my thirst for wisdom; it was my memories—or rather, my lack of connection to them. When I recalled moments from my past, it felt as if I were watching someone else's life—like a movie I had once seen but never lived. I could see the images, but they carried no familiarity, no sense of *me* within them. Who was I before this? And who had I become?

As I worked to reconnect with my body and shape a new life, something even more inexplicable began to unfold. I discovered gifts—abilities I had no recollection of ever having. I would envision something, and it would come to pass. I *knew* things about people without them telling me, sensing their deepest thoughts and emotions as if they were my own. When I confronted them about it, their reactions ranged from astonishment to unease. How could I know things they had never spoken aloud?

More than anything, I had the power to manifest. What I desired—what I deeply believed in—seemed to materialize effortlessly. This was not something I had been taught. It was as if a dormant part of me had awakened, rewriting the rules of my reality.

And yet, there remained one haunting mystery.

The night I spent in the hospital—the night everything changed—remains a complete blank. I didn't dream. I didn't experience anything I can remember. It is the only night of my life that is erased as if it never existed. I often wonder: *Was something taken from me? Or was something given?*

It took me nearly a decade to begin uncovering the truth about what happened that night. But one thing was undeniable—who I *had* been was gone, and whoever I had become was only beginning to reveal itself.

During those years, I became an avid seeker, devouring books on the unseen, the mystical, the extraordinary. I was drawn to anything that hinted at answers beyond what the physical world could explain. One day, I found myself wandering through a bookstore. It felt like an ordinary visit—until a book fell from the shelf, landing right at my feet.

The moment I saw it, I *knew*.

It wasn't random. It wasn't a coincidence. It was calling me.

The book was *Strangers Among Us* by Ruth Montgomery.

I took it home and immediately began reading, unable to put it down. Every word pulled me deeper, each page stirring something in me that I couldn't yet name. I had assumed it was about extraterrestrials, but I was in for a much greater revelation.

The book spoke of higher realms—of souls that could *walk in* and take over the body and life of another soul who had chosen to transition.

They called them *walk-ins*. A term I had never heard before.

And yet, in that instant, I *knew*.

I understood what had happened on that lost night, I couldn't remember—the night I didn't dream. The exchange had taken place in that void. I *felt* it in my bones, in the very core of my being. I finally recognized what I was.

I was a *walk-in*.

Suddenly, everything made sense.

But clarity doesn't always mean immediate acceptance. It would take many more years—*and two more near-death experiences*—before I fully embraced the gifts that had awakened within me that day. My spiritual journey had begun, though I didn't yet realize just how profound it would be.

Now, I see with absolute clarity—everything I endured was preparing me for my true work: guiding others through their own transformation. Because of this journey, I connect on a soul level, holding space as others awaken and begin to remember who they truly are. I bring forth wisdom that flows effortlessly from divine truth, illuminating the path for those ready to step into their highest selves.

Through coaching, speaking, and teaching, I help others remember who they *really* are—just as I remembered who *I* am.

Everything that happened in those years shaped me into the *spiritual architect* I am today. I walk this path with full intention, knowing that my purpose is to illuminate the way for others.

\*\*\*

*Esther Jone-Alley,*
*Spiritual Architect*
www.estherjones-alley
https://www.facebook.com/EstherJAlley
https://www.linkedin.com/in/estherjonesalley/
https://www.instagram.com/estherjonesalley/
https://www.youtube.com/@EstherJoneslifecoach

# Jen Fontanilla

Jen Fontanilla is a TEDx speaker, bestselling author, and leading voice in the AI-driven creative economy. With 20 years in finance and 25 years in design, she merges money mindset, creativity, and AI innovation, helping graphic designers, AI-driven artists, and creative entrepreneurs unlock their full financial potential.

As a Certified Money Coach (CMC)®, former financial advisor, and accomplished graphic designer who has worked with industry giants like Disney, Sony, U.S. Air Force ROTC, Target, and Nintendo, Jen deeply understands the challenges creatives face with pricing, financial confidence, and industry shifts. Her work empowers creatives to break free from scarcity, charge confidently, and thrive—without burnout, hustle, or compromise.

A recognized thought leader, Jen has been featured in *The Wall Street Times, The Los Angeles Tribune, Artists Weekly,* and *She Is AI Magazine*. She shares insights globally on AI's future in creative industries, financial empowerment for creatives, and how universal laws shape abundance, fostering a strong creative community.

Through her book *The Creative Code: A Creative Professional's Way to Happiness, Wealth, and Joy* and her money mindset work, Jen helps creatives build wealth with ease, fun, and passion—while doing what they love. Whether through speaking, writing, or coaching, she is dedicated to helping creatives rewrite their money stories and create thriving, prosperous futures.

# The AI Shift: Rewriting the Rules for Women in Creativity and Wealth

By Jen Fontanilla

Remember when you were a little girl and how you dreamed of becoming absolutely anything you aspired to be? How exciting did it feel, how your heart lit up, and how easily joy and possibility filled your days? What happened to that little girl? Is she still inside you, guiding your dreams, creativity, and sense of wonder—or did you let the world convince you that her dreams weren't realistic, or worse, weren't even possible? We've all had moments when our childhood enthusiasm got buried beneath practicality, expectations, and doubt. But deep down, that curious, joyful, creative little girl is still there, waiting to come out and play again.

When I heard about AI toward the end of 2022, I was far from that little girl's playful curiosity. I rolled my eyes, thinking, "Great—another gimmick. Just another fad everyone's jumping on." (Insert major eye-roll.) It immediately brought me back to the frenzy around Clubhouse, where everyone scrambled to score that special invite, convinced it was the next big thing until it wasn't.

People buzzed around me about ChatGPT, OpenAI, prompts, artificial intelligence—blah, blah, blah. My initial reaction was pure resistance. Ugh, that's another thing I have to learn. Whatever, it'll fade away.

Boy, was I wrong.

Fast-forward to today—AI is here, reshaping industries and unlocking new opportunities. Most importantly, it's offering women a powerful new way to step up, speak up, and close the persistent gender gap in tech and creative fields. With AI, women are not just participants but leaders, shaping the future of creativity and technology.

By 2030, AI will add $15.7 trillion to the global economy (PwC, 2023). Yet, women make up just 22% of AI professionals, though companies with top-tier gender diversity are 25% more likely to outperform financially (McKinsey, 2023). That's a problem. Women aren't any less creative, capable, or tech-savvy than men, so why such a vast disparity?

It's more than just numbers. For years, many talented, ambitious women have been talked over in meetings, overlooked for promotions, or dismissed as not "technical enough." Too often, we hear, "Stay in your lane." The result? Countless amazing women, brimming with creativity and innovation, play small or feel invisible.

How do I know? Every virtual summit I've attended that features women at the forefront of AI includes stories of struggle. Panel after panel, women share their experiences of being dismissed, doubted, or outright excluded. Yet, they kept going and are now in charge of reshaping the industry for the next generation of women in tech and creativity.

AI is a new playground. It's changing how creative industries operate—helping businesses integrate AI tools, work smarter, and create more efficiently. But the most exciting shift for creatives is this: AI allows us to bring ideas to life that were once impossible—or, at the very least, would have taken hours, days, or even weeks to execute.

Now, we can create complex designs, generate art, and edit visuals in minutes—tasks that once required painstaking effort. This frees us to focus on creativity, storytelling, and innovation. AI isn't replacing imagination—it's accelerating creative dreams into reality.

And who excels at imagination and creativity? Women do. Women aren't just entering AI—they're revolutionizing the dialogue. It's time to stop feeling overlooked and start owning this opportunity. Your voice matters, your ideas are valuable, and your influence is significant.

Whenever I use AI imaginatively, I feel like that little girl again—the one who spent hours coloring, painting, and getting lost in her imagination without worrying about what others might think. AI has become my digital playground, reigniting my sense of joy and possibility. It reminded me how important it is to nurture that childlike enthusiasm and creativity, doing work that lights me up from the inside out.

AI is not just another tool; it's a source of endless creative exploration and genuine joy. It's an imaginative space that reconnects me daily with the simple fun and fulfillment I felt as a child. It's become exactly what that little girl inside me always dreamed of.

## **AI as a Creative Partner**

Many fear AI will replace humans, but the truth is those who embrace AI will replace those who don't. AI enhances creativity by refining ideas, accelerating workflows, and freeing time for what matters most. It's not here to replace us but to amplify us.

If you've been hesitant about trying AI, start with something simple. Test an AI tool in a low-pressure, playful way—let curiosity lead. You might find that AI isn't intimidating at all. Instead, it can become your secret weapon for unlocking creativity, efficiency, and success. The beautiful thing about AI is that it's flexible—it can adapt to your needs, whether you're a designer, writer, or digital artist. You don't have to be an AI expert to integrate it into your workflow.

AI is revolutionizing creative work, making bringing ideas to life and streamlining workflows easier. The AI industry is projected to contribute $15.7 trillion to the global economy by 2030 (PwC, 2023). This isn't just a trend—it's the future. Whether generating new design concepts, assisting with writing, or enhancing photography, AI transforms how creatives work. Take Adobe Photoshop, for example. Before AI, I spent hours carefully crafting backgrounds and retouching images pixel by pixel. Now, generative AI instantly creates multiple stunning backgrounds. Suddenly, I have more options to show clients and more time for everything else. AI hasn't taken anything from me—it's leveraged and expanded my creativity, making my work even more potent.

**Here are a few ways women are already using AI today:**

**AI in Graphic Design & Branding**

For designers, AI tools can help create mood boards, generate ideas, and automate tedious tasks. Platforms like Midjourney, Adobe Firefly, and DALL·E allow designers to instantly create concept visuals, cutting down hours of manual sketching and brainstorming.

For example, instead of spending hours refining multiple versions of a brand concept, AI can generate logo ideas, background textures, and social media graphics in minutes. This speeds up the creative process and allows for more experimentation and refinement.

### AI for Writers, Authors & Content Creators

AI is becoming an essential tool for writers. It helps with brainstorming, outlining, and improving writing. While it doesn't replace an author's unique voice, AI enhances the creative process by offering suggestions and helping overcome writer's block.

For instance, if you're struggling to start a blog post or book chapter, AI-powered tools like ChatGPT, Jasper, and Claude AI can provide a rough draft based on your ideas. This eliminates the frustration of staring at a blank page, giving you a foundation to build upon and refine.

### AI in Photography & Digital Art

Photographers and digital artists use AI to enhance images, streamline editing, and push the boundaries of creative expression. Tools like Adobe Sensei, Runway, and Topaz Labs can remove backgrounds, upscale low-resolution images, and precisely adjust lighting and color.

AI quickly enhances photos, freeing artists to focus on their creative vision instead of spending hours on tedious retouching. AI-assisted digital tools also offer new creative possibilities, making complex effects and photorealistic renderings more accessible.

### **Ethical AI Use: The Responsibility is in Our Hands**

AI is here to stay, transforming how we work and create—but with innovation comes responsibility. As creatives, we're not just users of AI; we shape how it's used. This raises an important question: *How do we ensure AI is ethical?*

Let's address the elephant in the room: "Is using AI cheating?" Many creatives worry—*Is AI stealing from artists? Taking jobs? Undermining originality?* These concerns are valid, but AI's ethics depend on its users, just as with any tool. Just as photography didn't erase painting, and dig, intention, and integrity: ital art didn't eliminate traditional techniques, AI enhances creativity rather than replacing it. Ethical AI use comes down to transparency

**Give credit where it's due.** Acknowledge AI's role in your work. Transparency doesn't diminish creativity—it builds trust.

**Use AI as a tool, not a replacement.** AI can refine ideas and speed up workflows, but your skills and vision remain the driving force.

**Avoid direct plagiarism.** Some AI tools generate content based on existing work. Instead of copying, use AI-generated ideas as inspiration and make them your own.

**Advocate for fair AI practices.** Support ethical AI development and choose platforms that respect original creators.

AI isn't inherently good or bad—it's a tool. How we use it determines whether it creates harm or opens new pathways.

**Fear vs. Possibility: Choosing the Creative Path Forward**

This fear isn't new. Society has long conditioned women to undervalue their work, hesitate to charge for their value, and feel conflicted about making money from creativity. Many artists see their talent as a gift rather than a service, believing monetizing it makes them inauthentic or a "sellout."

But creativity has value. Just because something comes easily doesn't mean it isn't worth charging for. No one questions paying an engineer or doctor—so why do creatives? The belief that struggle makes creativity "real" has long held artists and designers back. It's time to release that outdated narrative and create a new reality where your creativity is recognized, valued, and financially rewarding.

AI is more than a tool—it's a gateway. It opens doors, creates income, and allows creatives to charge for their ideas and expertise in new ways. Prosperity teachers like Catherine Ponder, Florence

Scovel Shinn, and Wallace D. Wattles taught that abundance is a God-given birthright. When you fully embrace your talents and gifts and allow them to generate wealth, you're not taking them from others—you're stepping into the natural flow of abundance without guilt.

Creativity isn't meant to be given away—it can sustain and enrich your life. You can confidently make money doing what you love—without guilt. What if AI wasn't just about learning tech—but about creating wealth from creativity, freely and unapologetically? You deserve to thrive in this space.

## The Money Conversation We Need to Have

AI is reshaping how we create, earn, and step into financial empowerment. But beyond the innovation, we need to have an honest conversation about what money really means. Money is more than numbers; it's freedom, choices, and the ability to shape one's life.

Many creatives—especially women—struggle with money. We undervalue our work, hesitate to charge fairly, and even feel guilty for profiting from what we love. We're taught that passion and profit shouldn't mix and that making money from creativity somehow taints it. But here's the shift: You deserve to thrive—precisely as you are, creating incredible work with your gifts.

Women-owned businesses generate $1.8 trillion in the U.S. but receive just 2% of venture capital funding (NAWBO, 2023). AI is set to add trillions to the economy, making it a powerful gateway for women to build wealth on their terms. AI presents an unprecedented chance for women to create, innovate, and build thriving businesses—on their terms.

Mastering AI creatively makes your work uniquely valuable—something clients can't easily replicate. You're not just a creator—you're a pioneer using cutting-edge tools to deliver extraordinary results and confidently charge what you deserve. I've seen this firsthand—women using AI to launch thriving businesses, lead as consultants, and build digital agencies. They're monetizing AI-driven skills through workshops, courses, and high-value services.

Abundance isn't just about earning more—it's about living fully, confidently, and joyfully. AI can be your vehicle for the abundance you deserve.

## Where to Start: Your AI Journey

You might think: *Okay, Jen, I get it—AI is powerful, but where do I start?*

I felt the same way. But you don't have to be an expert to succeed with AI. It's okay to start small, explore at your own pace, and build confidence over time. The best way to start? Stay curious, be open, and let yourself experiment without pressure.

**Play with AI.** Curiosity is your superpower. Try tools like ChatGPT, Perplexity, or Midjourney—there is no pressure; just explore. Experiment with prompts, and expect some wild results. Suppose your AI images have six fingers, twisted legs, or eyes looking in different directions—congrats! You're on the right track! Laugh, learn, and tweak your inputs. Every "ugly" experiment sharpens your vision and deepens your understanding.

**Find your tribe—women exploring AI creatively.** Surround yourself with others who are also experimenting with AI. Join groups, forums, and communities focused on AI learning like *She Is AI* (www.sheisaimagazine.com). Your community isn't just for support—it's your inspiration, motivation, and space to exchange ideas. The more you immerse yourself in conversations around AI, the faster you'll grow. One of the best places to connect with women AI trailblazers is LinkedIn.

**Find a mentor—or become one.** Learn from those ahead of you whose work and insights resonate with you. Teaching others deepens your expertise and expands opportunities. And if you've already picked up valuable AI skills, don't downplay what you know. Share it. There are women out there who are just starting and could benefit from your insight.

**Embrace visibility—share your journey.** Showcasing AI projects isn't just about attracting possibilities—it's about owning your growth. AI sharpens creative thinking, making you more valuable in ways you might not realize yet.

You don't need all the answers before you begin. Start small, stay curious, and don't shy away from the messy, imperfect, funny moments. They're proof you're moving forward.

## The Mindset Shift That Changes Everything

As exciting as the practical and creative opportunities are, your mindset is another key to genuinely thriving on your AI journey. This isn't just a nice-to-have, fluffy concept; it's foundational. I dedicate an entire chapter to this in my book, *The Creative Code: The Creative Professional's Way to Happiness, Wealth and Joy*, because understanding and aligning with these universal laws can dramatically change your results.

You might think, "Wait, did we just go woo-woo?" Oh, heck yeah, we did! These universal laws aren't just theory—they're powerful tools to shift your mindset and open yourself to absolute abundance and success.

Take the **Law of Polarity**; it reminds us that every obstacle holds equal or more significant opportunity. If AI feels daunting or frustrating, there's something incredible waiting on the other side. Instead of feeling stuck or discouraged, ask yourself, "What's the hidden opportunity here?" That simple shift in perspective can unlock possibilities you haven't even considered.

Then there's the **Law of Increase**, which says that what you appreciate and focus on multiplies. Celebrate every step of your AI journey—the small wins, the learning moments, and, yes, even those quirky, imperfect outcomes. By appreciating your progress, you signal that you're ready for more abundance and opportunity.

The **Law of Gratitude** takes this even further. When you genuinely appreciate your experiences, community, and even your hilarious AI mistakes, you naturally create energy that attracts more things to be grateful for. Gratitude elevates your vibration and opens the door to limitless growth.

Finally, the **Law of Attraction** reminds us that the energy and attitude you put out will shape what you receive in return.

Approaching AI with openness, optimism, and curiosity attracts experiences and opportunities aligned with your vision of success.

Aligning your mindset with abundance and deservingness ensures your journey with AI is smoother, more rewarding, and infinitely more joyful. Everything changes when you shift your thinking about AI, work, and value.

## **It's Never Too Late to Reinvent Yourself**

Maybe you're still thinking, *"Is this possible for me?"* If you don't come from a tech or creative background, thriving with AI might feel far-fetched. But let me assure you—it's totally possible. Women from all walks of life are proving it every single day.

I know incredible women in their 50s and 60s who've completely reinvented their careers using AI tools. Although they weren't professional designers or tech experts beforehand, they saw the potential AI offered and went for it. Today, they run thriving digital marketing agencies, host packed workshops, and consult with businesses that value their creative skills in different industries. They didn't let age, inexperience, or self-doubt stop them. Instead, they chose courage over fear.

I've also seen firsthand how AI accelerates success. Integrating AI into my workflow, I created a financial strategy to pay off debt, write and market my book, and create engaging content faster. AI didn't replace my creativity—it amplified it. It opened doors I hadn't considered and helped me achieve my once-only-dreamed-of financial goals.

A skeptical friend embraced AI and, within months, transformed her business into an AI-powered branding service provider. Her income, confidence, and creativity soared.

AI isn't just a tool—it's a catalyst for transformation. It doesn't discriminate based on age, background, or experience. It rewards curiosity, courage, and the willingness to explore. If you're still hesitating, remember these women—and remember me. We're proof that it's never too late, you're never too inexperienced, and the creative life you want is within reach.

## **Step Forward—The World Is Ready for You**

I started this chapter by admitting I was skeptical about AI. I dismissed it as another trendy distraction that would fade as quickly as it appeared. But embracing AI changed the trajectory of my creativity, finances, and life. And now, I want the same for you.

AI isn't just a tool—it's a gateway to creativity, growth, and financial empowerment. The women you've read about in this chapter didn't wait for permission, nor should you. Whether you're just starting or already exploring AI, trust that you are exactly where you need to be. The key isn't knowing everything—it's being willing to begin.

You don't have to be fearless. You don't have to be an expert. You have to be curious enough to try. Find mentors, join communities, and step forward even when uncertain. Laugh at the quirks, embrace the surprises, and celebrate every small win. The gender gap in AI isn't going to close itself—it changes when women like you step up, speak out, and claim the space that has always been yours.

So go ahead.

Play.

Experiment.

Create boldly.

AI is here, and so are you.

And trust me—the world is more than ready for your brilliance.

*\*\*\**

## CONNECT WITH JEN

Learn more at www.jenmoneycoach.com and follow her at @jenmoneycoach.

**LinkedIn:** www.linkedin.com/in/jenmoneycoach

**Instagram:** www.instagram.com/jenmoneycoach

**Facebook:** www.facebook.com/jenmoneycoach

**FREE GIFT- Money Mediation:**
https://bit.ly/TheChangeFREEGIFT

Struggle with pricing, negotiating, or asking for money? This guide helps creatives overcome discomfort, value their work, and confidently pitch.

# Stacy Phoenix Freeman

Stacy Phoenix didn't just find confidence—she fought for it. Born in Salem, Oregon, and raised in Lowell, MA, she grew up watching her Cambodian immigrant parents work tirelessly to build a better life. That resilience became part of her DNA, but nothing could have prepared her for the moment her world fell apart.

After her divorce, she was lost, heartbroken, and suddenly a single mother to her one-year-old daughter. With no clear path forward, she refused to give up. Instead, she rebuilt—one step, one lesson, one act of courage at a time.

Her journey led her to spirituality, where she discovered Reiki and the power of energy healing. When her Chakra Therapy teacher told her, "You'd make an incredible coach," something inside her shifted. She followed the call, built her business from the ground up, and never looked back. Now, from her home in New Hampshire, she's known as the best Confidence Coach on the East Coast, helping aspiring actors and models step into their power and own the spotlight.

With 12 certifications—including NLP Master, Reiki Master, and Hypnotherapy—Stacy blends deep, transformational coaching with a nurturing approach. Her clients don't just gain confidence; they find a safe space to heal, grow, and thrive.

Beyond coaching, Stacy loves singing, dancing, painting, and photography. A pescatarian and health enthusiast, her greatest joy is being a mother to her daughter—the brightest light in her life.

Confidence isn't just something she teaches—it's something she lives.

# From Darkness to Light:
# My Journey to Freedom and Confidence

## *By Stacy Phoenix Freeman*

I never thought I'd be here. Living this life. Feeling this free.

Looking back, there were so many moments where I could've been lost forever—swallowed by pain, buried in silence. But something in me refused to give up. Maybe it was my spirit. Maybe it was my daughter. Maybe it was the Universe, whispering, Not yet. You're meant for more.

**A Childhood Shaped by Silence**

I was born in Salem, Oregon, to two resilient Cambodian immigrant parents who had survived unthinkable trauma and came to America for a better life. We later moved to Lowell, Massachusetts, where I grew up. My parents worked hard, loved deeply, and did their best with what they had. Their strength shaped me—but even their love couldn't protect me from everything.

When I was six years old, someone I trusted crossed a boundary no child should ever endure. I didn't understand it at the time. I just knew something had changed in me. That moment planted a seed of silence and shame that would take decades to unearth.

So I poured myself into perfection. In school, I was the nerd—the smart girl. Straight As, peer leader, honor roll. By eighth grade, I was President of the National Junior Honor Society. I was driven, well-liked, and on the surface, thriving.

By seventh and eighth grade, I had somehow become one of the popular girls. But popularity never healed pain. I learned early that attention doesn't equal love, and success doesn't equal peace.

**Love, Betrayal, and First Heartbreak**

In high school, I didn't run with a specific crowd. I had a few great friends and a big heart. Then came my first real boyfriend—my first taste of love. It was passionate, dramatic, and unhealthy.

We were on and off, back and forth. And in the end, he betrayed me by falling for my cousin.

I remember the humiliation. The gut-punch of discovering that the person I gave my heart to had given pieces of it away behind my back. I didn't just lose a boyfriend—I lost trust.

I internalized the pain. I told myself it was because I wasn't enough. Not pretty enough. Not fun enough. Not lovable enough. That single belief haunted me for years.

## A Marriage That Broke Me—and Gave Me My Greatest Gift

My next relationship eventually led to marriage. He seemed different—grounded, mature, safe. I thought I was finally building a solid future. But it didn't take long for the emotional and physical abuse to show.

It was subtle at first. A quiet erosion of my confidence. Controlling behaviors masked as "protection." Blame disguised as "truth." I didn't recognize it for what it was—until I was deep in it.

Still, I tried to make it work. I told myself I could fix it if I just tried harder, loved harder, stayed longer. I ignored the parts of me that were slowly disappearing.

Then I got pregnant.

When I found out I was having a daughter, something inside me stirred. I looked at the life I was living, the energy in our home, the fear under the surface—and I knew I couldn't raise a child in that.

But I stayed. Because leaving felt impossible. I convinced myself things would change. That love was supposed to be hard.

After my daughter was born, the cracks turned into craters. We barely got along. When we did, it was in public—to keep up appearances. The final straw was infidelity. Again.

This time, I walked.

I moved back in with my parents, holding my one-year-old daughter in one arm and my broken heart in the other. I was exhausted. Depressed. Defeated. I had no idea what came next.

## The Promise That Changed Everything

One night, sitting alone in my childhood bedroom, I looked over at my sleeping daughter and broke into tears. I'd never felt so lost.

But then, I heard my own voice whisper:

I don't know where I'm going. But I know I want to be happy. I want to be the best mother I can be. And we both deserve more than this.

That was the moment I decided to stop surviving and start living.

## A Click, A Calling, and the Start of Healing

A few nights later, I was online, searching for anything to pull me out of the darkness. Crystals. Energy work. Spiritual healing. Then I saw it: a simple Google ad about Reiki.

I didn't know what it was. But I clicked on it. Something about it spoke to me. I followed the nudge and found a Reiki center near me. I signed up for Level 1 training, nervous but hopeful.

That single decision changed everything.

In that first Reiki class, I felt something I hadn't felt in years: peace.

It wasn't loud or dramatic. It was soft, gentle, familiar. Like my soul had finally come home.

I kept going. Reiki led me to meditation, the Universal Laws, energetic healing, and soul alignment. I began to uncover the parts of me I had abandoned—my light, my voice, my truth.

Eventually, I became a Reiki Master. I added certifications in NLP, Chakra Therapy, Hypnotherapy, and more. With each new layer, I healed deeper.

And slowly, I realized—I didn't just want to heal. I wanted to help others heal too.

## The Birth of My Coaching Business

During the pandemic, when the world stood still, I decided to fully step into my calling. I launched my coaching business with a dream and a laptop. I had no roadmap, no investors—just intuition and faith.

Within six months, I manifested my first six-figure job. I was doing what I loved, helping people transform, guiding them home to themselves.

But the more light you carry, the more you attract both love and shadows. I experienced spiritual attacks—jealousy, dark energy, psychic interference. I had to learn to protect my space, my peace, my purpose.

And then, life threw me one of its most painful tests.

## Losing My Light—and Finding a New One

My grandmother passed away.

She was my caretaker growing up, the one who made me feel safe when the world didn't. Her love was unconditional. Her presence was my anchor.

When she died, I felt like my own light went out. I spiraled—emotionally, mentally, spiritually. I took time off from my business to grieve. I disconnected from almost everyone.

But grief, as painful as it is, became a sacred teacher.

It stripped me down to the rawest version of myself.

And it was from that rawness that I began to rebuild.

## The Rise After the Fall

I went all in.

I worked two full-time jobs. I ran my business. I raised my daughter. I sacrificed my social life. I cut ties with toxic family members and so-called friends who didn't honor my healing.

I was bullied, emotionally abused, and betrayed by people I once trusted. And I had to learn that love isn't always enough to keep people in your life.

Letting go hurt. But staying would've hurt more.

So I chose myself.

I forgave the people who hurt me. But more importantly, I forgave me. For the times I ignored my intuition. For the times I hurt others from my own pain. For the times I abandoned myself.

And I stopped numbing.

I stopped drinking. I stopped doing drugs. I let go of the substances that once felt like survival but were actually self-sabotage. I don't drink anymore. I don't escape. I feel. I heal.

Sobriety brought me clarity. Power. Wholeness.

**The Life I Live Now**

Today, I coach incredible clients—aspiring actors, models, creatives, and healers. I help them reconnect to their confidence, purpose, and light.

I travel when I want. I speak my truth. I laugh with my daughter. I dance. I dream. I live.

And I'm still healing. Still growing. Still becoming.

But I'm doing it with clarity. With love. With intention.

I made a promise to my daughter and to myself:

We will be happy. We will be free.

And now, we are.

**To You, My Reader**

If you're holding this book in your hands and wondering if your pain has a purpose—let me be the proof.

You are not broken.

You are not too late.

You are not too far gone.

You are becoming.

You are the light you've been searching for.

The strength is already inside you.

The confidence is already within you.

You just have to choose yourself—one brave breath at a time.

Your next chapter begins now.

And I hope it's the most beautiful one yet.

***

**Contact:**

Website: stacyphoenix.com

Instagram: @stacyphoenixcoaching

Facebook: https://www.facebook.com/share/1FpsKJZBXE/?mibextid=wwXIfr

YouTube: https://www.youtube.com/@stacyphoenix

TikTok: https://www.tiktok.com/@stacyphoenixcoaching?_t=ZT-8v7ZmXG9KaE&_r=1

@stacyphoenixcoaching

LinkedIn: https://www.linkedin.com/in/stacy-phoenix-b49151329?utm_source=share&utm_campaign=share_via&utm_content=profile&utm_medium=ios_app

# Halley Élise

Halley Élise is a Transformational Speaker, Empowerment Psychic, and Intuitive Mentor with over three decades of experience guiding individuals toward personal mastery. From childhood, she possessed an innate ability to perceive beyond the visible—a gift that evolved into a lifelong journey of awakening, teaching, and empowering others.

Blending sacred wisdom with intuitive knowledge, Halley's approach is rooted in the Alchemy of Being—the process of dissolving conditioned limitations and unlocking infinite potential. She teaches that every person is born with inner gifts and a direct link to Divine wisdom awaiting conscious activation.

A certified clinical hypnotherapist, ordained minister, and energy practitioner, she has developed transformative programs such as the Psychic Apprenticeship Program© and the Master Intuitive Intelligence Training Certification. Through meditation, breathwork, and sacred ritual, she guides others to elevate their vibration, awaken heightened intuition, and embody their most powerful form.

Her expertise has been featured across radio, television, and international publications, inspiring seekers worldwide.

"Transformation is not about becoming something new—it is about remembering what you have always been."

# The Awakening of Egypt Gato
## A Parable Inspired by the Sacred Alchemy of Being

### By Halley Elise

The Campus of Forever-More stood as a testament to time itself. Towering, ancient trees with vast canopies filtered sunlight through their boughs, painting unusual patterns below—whispers of venerated secrets for those prepared to listen. The very air pulsed with the wisdom of the Divine. Winding, innumerable paths meandered through the grounds, leading seekers and non-seekers alike—not just toward destinations but toward revelations within themselves.

Egypt Gato arrived at this hallowed place carrying the weight of an unknown past. A child abandoned before he could form memories.

He had been left on the sun-drenched streets of Cairo, swaddled in fabric, no more than four months old. A compassionate woman, soft-eyed and full of grace, had found him and immediately recognized something in his eyes… a spark that others had overlooked. She named him Egypt, an echo of his origins. Yet, despite her warmth, a profound void lingered within him, a sense of never truly belonging, of being unanchored in the vast expanse of his existence.

Impelled by an inexplicable pull, Egypt found himself standing before The Luminaire—an irregularly shaped dormitory built of stones that seemed to glow from within, its presence mystical and humming with unseen frequencies. It was said to predate the university itself. Its walls vibrated with stories untold, waiting for the right moment to be heard.

Within The Luminaire, Egypt encountered two unexpected individuals—souls unlike any he had ever met. Shaylan McGhee carried an air of timelessness. His streaked silver hair and piercing blue eyes betrayed wisdom beyond ordinary lifetimes. Every word he spoke carried profound significance, distilled as though from Divine Truth itself.

EffieKiki Larouge was a force of nature—fluid yet unwavering, warm yet unrelenting. She possessed the look of a celestial heroine whose origin was impossible to determine. Though only three years his senior, she held the rank of High Master. Her ability to see beyond facades and into the fire of one's essence left those she encountered astonished, stripped bare of illusion.

From the moment they met, it was clear: They had been waiting for him. Upon entering their shared space, Egypt was drawn to an emerald green, three-wicked candle burning on the windowsill. Its flames moved with an odd, unseen rhythm—a silent dance to a song unheard.

One evening, as the candlelight flickered, he found himself entranced.

"You often lose yourself in thought," EffieKiki observed, stepping closer, the candle's flame reflected in her blue-green eyes. Egypt shrugged. "It's easier to converse with the silent."

She leaned in, a playful smile on her lips. "Are they truly silent, or have you yet to understand their language?"

Shaylan's gaze met Egypt's, his expression unreadable. "There is much you hear but have chosen to ignore."

Confusion clouded Egypt's face. "I don't understand what you mean." A knowing look passed between them.

"In time," Shaylan murmured, "you will."

The Tunnel and the Whisper of the Divine

That night, sleep eluded Egypt. Something unseen beckoned.

Wandering the campus, he followed an unknown pull, his steps leading him beyond the cultivated gardens—past the blooming lavender, roses, and daffodils—until he reached the edge of the wild forest. The air thickened, heavy with frankincense, sandalwood, and bergamot, the scent awakening memories he did not yet recognize. The forest stirred, vines parting to reveal an ancient tunnel, its entrance buried beneath the embrace of gnarled roots. A whisper, soft yet commanding, wove through the air: "Enter."

A cold sweat beaded on his brow. Shadows of self-doubt stirred, voices from his past rising in unison—fears long buried, insecurities long accepted. But beneath the noise, a deeper voice—one not of fear but of truth—resonated within him. Stand. Take what is yours to claim.

He stepped inside.

The Labyrinth of the Omnipotent Soul

Darkness swallowed him—not an absence of light, but a living force pulsing with energy.

Shadows coalesced into figures from his past. A boy, his younger self, stepped forward, eyes wide with longing. "Why was I abandoned?" the child asked. "How can you find your path when you don't know where you began?" The weight of the question pressed against Egypt. He had spent years searching for identity, feeling like a leaf carried by the wind—directionless, unrooted. And then, he remembered. EffieKiki's teachings. The breath.

He inhaled deeply, slow and steady. The air filled his lungs, cool and anchoring. He held the breath. He released. Again. Again. With each breath, the shadows receded. The tunnel, once ominous, shifted—transforming into a space of revelation. "Our worth is not defined by our beginnings," Egypt whispered, gazing at his younger self. "It is shaped by our choices."

The child's form shimmered, then merged with him. A wave of energy surged through him—integration. Acceptance. When he emerged from the tunnel, the world had changed. Or rather—he had changed.

The Dreaming Labyrinth and the Hall of Mirrors

Weeks passed in a blur of alchemy and awakening. Egypt immersed himself in the sacred knowledge, his senses sharpening, his perception expanding.

One evening, EffieKiki handed him a worn parchment. A hand-drawn map. A labyrinth.

"The Labyrinth of the Omnipotent Soul," Shaylan said. "It must be walked in the realm beyond waking." That night, guided by the unseen, Egypt entered The Dreaming Labyrinth. The paths twisted not just through space but through time.

At the heart of the labyrinth, he stood before a great hall of mirrors. Each reflection showed a different version of himself. Some wise. Some broken. Some lost. Some found.

A voice, his own, yet not his own—whispered:

"Which path is yours this time?" And then—understanding. "Not one path. All paths. They are all me." He touched the mirror. It did not reflect. It smiled. And then—shattered into dust.

The Return and the Unfolding of Destiny

Egypt awoke with a start. Then, breath steadied, heart quieted. Transformed. He sat up. The candle burned as always, its flames unmoving. Silent. Expectant. Shaylan and EffieKiki stood in the doorway, their expressions knowing.

"You walked the labyrinth," Shaylan stated. Egypt met their gaze. "And I found myself." EffieKiki smiled, radiant. "That is the only destination that ever mattered." The air pulsed, electric with knowing. Egypt had not merely stepped onto his path. He had become it.

The change was not immediate, nor was it loud. It was subtle, like the first rays of dawn creeping over the horizon, shifting not just Egypt Gato's awareness but his very being. His once light carrot-colored hair had deepened to a luminous auburn, the sun catching strands of gold and copper within it. His frame, once lanky and almost frail, had transformed. There was a strength in his shoulders now, a quiet power in the way he moved. He was taller, his presence more grounded and inevitable, as if the earth responded to him differently.

Shaylan noticed first.

"You're no longer walking like a man seeking answers," he remarked one morning as they stood in the sacred gardens. "You move as though you know they are already within you."

Egypt hadn't been aware of the shift, but now he was. The way his footsteps carried weight. The way people turned their heads as he passed.

He exhaled, watching the mist rise from the morning dew, feeling the delicate threads of energy that wove between all things.

EffieKiki approached, placing a warm hand on his back. "You've begun to embody it," she said.

"Embody what?" Egypt asked. "The alchemy of being."

She knelt, tracing her fingers through the cool soil beneath an olive tree, cupping the earth in her palm. "This," she murmured, "is just dirt to most. But when tended with intention, it becomes fertile ground for life. When blessed, it becomes sacred. And when understood, it becomes a mirror for the soul." Egypt watched as she let the earth slip through her fingers, each grain falling like sand through the unseen hourglass of time.

"Everything we touch," Shaylan added, "everything we do, becomes alchemy when infused with presence and purpose." That day, Egypt was given his next teaching—one that had nothing to do with books or ancient texts. It was about the sacred within the mundane. How the way one wakes in the morning can set the course for an entire day.

How lighting a candle with intention can illuminate more than just a room. How drinking water, with gratitude, can purify more than just the body. It was the practice of ritual. Not ritual as ceremony alone, but as a way of life. And as he embraced it, the world responded.

The Subtle Magnetism of Presence

At first, it was barely noticeable. A glance held a moment longer. A stranger's smile in passing. The way people seemed to lean toward him, drawn without understanding why. It wasn't just his physical transformation—though his striking auburn hair, his strengthened frame, and the quiet intensity in his eyes made him impossible to ignore. It was something deeper.

Something felt, not seen.

One afternoon, while sitting beneath the ancient oak tree in the courtyard, a student approached him hesitantly. "I don't know why I feel like telling you this," she began, shifting uneasily. "But I… I feel lost. Like I don't belong, not anywhere." Egypt looked at her—

not just at her face, but beyond it. He didn't rush to speak. He didn't fill the space with empty words. Instead, he let silence do its work.

And then, gently, he said, "You don't have to know where you belong. Just start by belonging to yourself." The girl's eyes filled with tears, as if those words had unlocked something within her. Egypt hadn't intended to mentor anyone. But people kept coming. Day by day, one by one, they found him—strangers drawn to something within him.

Not because he sought to teach. But because he had become the embodiment of what they longed for. Certainty. Stillness.

Awakening.

It wasn't long before his presence stirred even those in positions of power. Professors took notice. Some were fascinated. Others were wary. "Have you seen him?" one whispered in passing. "There's something about the way he speaks. The way he listens." The Head Scholar of the university—an elderly man known for his skepticism—observed Egypt from afar before finally calling him into his chamber. "I have heard of you," he said, studying Egypt carefully.

Egypt did not bow. He did not shrink. He simply met the man's gaze, neither arrogant nor uncertain. "I am just a student," Egypt said. The Head Scholar narrowed his eyes. "No, you are something else entirely."

There was no accusation in his tone—only curiosity. Egypt simply waited. A long silence passed. Then, finally, the old man spoke. "I have studied the great philosophers, the mystics, the scientists of human nature. They all sought wisdom. But you—you move as if you have already found it."

Egypt smiled slightly. "Wisdom isn't something you find. It's something you live." The Head Scholar exhaled a slow breath as if seeing something he could not name. "Perhaps it is time," he murmured, "for a new way of seeing things." From that day, Egypt's influence expanded beyond Luminaire, beyond the halls of academia. Not because he forced it.

But because his being had become a mirror, reflecting what others had always known but had forgotten.

One evening, as he stood on the edge of the gardens, gazing at the sky, Shaylan approached.

"You are no longer who you were when you arrived," he observed.

Egypt inhaled deeply, feeling the air, the pulse of the earth beneath him, the stars above. "No," he agreed. "I am not."

EffieKiki emerged from the shadows, smiling. "And yet, you are more yourself than ever."

Egypt turned to them, feeling, for the first time, no need to ask any more questions. "Is there more?" he asked, not out of doubt but out of readiness. EffieKiki laughed. "There is always more." Shaylan nodded, stepping forward. "But the difference now, Egypt, is that you no longer seek it outside of yourself. You have become it." A gust of wind stirred, and for a moment, the flames of the three-wicked candle back in their chamber leaped high, casting elongated shadows against the walls. And as the night deepened, Egypt Gato stood, not as a student nor a seeker, but as an embodiment of the Alchemy of Being. His journey had not ended. It had only just begun.

The labyrinth pulsed around him, alive, shifting. He had come so far. Faced so much. And yet—the weight of the past still clung to him.

Through the mist, he saw himself as a child again.

Small. Vulnerable. Staring up at him with wide, questioning eyes.

"Why was I abandoned?" the boy asked. Egypt had already answered this before. He had already spoken of how his worth was not bound to his beginnings. But this time, the boy's voice wavered. His expression changed. "Why would you leave me behind?"

The words hit differently. Egypt's chest tightened. "I didn't," he whispered. "I am you."

The child shook his head. "No. You left me. You are leaving me." A storm of memories rushed through Egypt's mind: the safety of old doubts, the familiarity of uncertainty, and the ache of loneliness, once a constant companion.

The boy took a step back, fading into the mist. Egypt felt a pull, a powerful, magnetic urge to run after him. To hold onto what was known.

It would be so easy. To step back into uncertainty. To believe in his smallness. To stay lost. His breath caught. His hands clenched. His entire body screamed for the comfort of the old.

"Do not look back." A voice not from the labyrinth but from deep within his own being.

"If you chase him, you will become him again."

The boy's face flickered, his image breaking like water disturbed. Egypt closed his eyes, inhaled deeply… not to push the child away, but to embrace him differently.

"I am not leaving you," he whispered. "I am bringing you with me."

And with that, he stepped forward. The child did not disappear.

Instead, he merged.

For the first time, Egypt felt whole. And when he opened his eyes, the labyrinth was no longer there.

Back in The Luminaire, the candle burned. Its three flames moved unnaturally, bending in directions that defied logic. Egypt sat before it, drawn in once more. Not just seeing it but feeling it. He had stared at this flame countless nights before. But this time, something shifted. The flames lengthened, pulsing as if whispering in a language of light. His vision blurred. Then sharpened.

He gasped. The air around him was no longer empty space—it was filled with patterns.

Golden spirals woven through everything. Threads of light coiled around the furniture, twisting in Fibonacci sequences. The very walls of the dorm breathed, moving in harmony with an unseen rhythm. Outside, the trees glowed. The sky pulsed in soft waves of energy. He turned to EffieKiki, and for the first time, he saw her aura—a luminous gold flickering like a star.

His breath caught as he turned to Shaylan, whose form radiated a deep silver-blue, his presence vast, like the night sky itself. Egypt's chest tightened, not in fear but in awe. This had always been here. He had simply not seen it. "Light," he murmured. His voice trembled. "Everything… is light." Shaylan smirked. "You finally see." EffieKiki placed a hand on his shoulder. "And now, you will never unsee." He blinked, shaking his head, the world slowly returning to its normal view, but not completely.

Something had shifted permanently. And Egypt had just received his first lesson in superconscious vision.

Word of Egypt's presence had spread. His transformation had become a quiet ripple throughout the university. People found themselves drawn to him. Not by force. Not by effort. Just by presence. One afternoon, a younger student, Joshua, approached him.

"I don't know what's wrong with me," Joshua confessed, rubbing his hands together nervously. "I feel… lost. I look in the mirror and don't recognize myself."

The candle's flame was no longer just fire. It was a teacher. Egypt considered him for a moment. Then, he gestured toward a nearby still-water pond. "Sit with me." Joshua hesitated, then obeyed.

Egypt pulled a small mirror from his pocket and handed it to him.

"Look into your own eyes," Egypt instructed. "Do not move. Do not look away. Just see."

Joshua exhaled, lifting the mirror hesitantly.

Seconds passed. Then minutes. At first, nothing. Then, something shifted. His own face seemed to change. The more he stared, the more his features blurred… morphed… expanded.

He saw himself older. Wiser. Stronger. Then, he saw himself younger. A child. Then, he saw himself as something more. Something infinite. Joshua gasped, nearly dropping the mirror. "What was that?" he whispered, his voice shaking. Egypt smiled. "That was you." Joshua's breath came in short bursts. "I don't…I don't… understand." "You will." Egypt rose, dusting off his clothes.

"Now that you've seen beyond yourself… you will never again be only what you once believed."

The boy stared at the mirror, his entire existence subtly but permanently altered.

Final Realization.

That evening, Egypt sat in solitude. The candle burned, its light familiar. But now, he understood.

He was no longer just a student. A seeker. A wanderer. He was becoming. A force. A guide. A living alchemy of all that he had learned.

Shaylan and EffieKiki entered the room and stood behind him. "You understand now," Shaylan said, though it was not a question.

Egypt nodded. "I do."

EffieKiki smiled softly. "Then tell me, Egypt Gato, what is the truth of transformation?" Egypt closed his eyes. When he opened them, the candle's flame reflected in his gaze, its wisdom now his own. "Transformation is not about becoming something new," he said, voice steady. "It is about remembering what we have always been." EffieKiki's smile widened. Shaylan crossed his arms. "Then you are ready." Egypt did not ask for what. He already knew. The three-wicked candle burned brighter, its flames rising high—an unspoken acknowledgment of what had just been sealed.

Egypt Gato had not merely changed. He had become.

***

For more information about Halley Élise

561.755.2166

Website: halleyelise.com

Instagram: @therealhalleyelise

Facebook: facebook.com/PsychicHalleyElise

LinkedIn: linkedin.com/in/halleyelise

YouTube: youtube.com/c/HalleyElise

Pinterest: pinterest.com/halleyelise

# Matt Orzech

Matt Orzech is a divorce recovery specialist. Uniquely qualified as a self-help addict, a real estate junkie, and a recovering divorce attorney, Matt is dedicated to changing individual's lives after divorce and other life transitions. Using his formal education, traditional counseling, church groups, self-help books, seminars, coaching, and life experiences, Matt crafted a master coaching practice to help others thrive after they survive. As CEO and Master Coach for *Freedom in Relationships*, he developed the *Triggers to Truth Program: Mastering your Emotional Intelligence so you can have Emotional Freedom*, which can guide you to a legendary life and epic relationships. Matt teaches that the quality of your life is ALL about the quality of your relationships: your relationship with your work, money, children, family, friends, spirituality, significant other, ex-significant others, health, and ultimately, the most important relationship of all, the relationship with yourself.

# From Triggers to Truth:
# Matt Orzech's Life Transformation After Divorce

## By Matt Orzech

I thought I had life figured out. As a real estate banker in the booming mid-2000s, I rode the wave of a housing market that seemed unstoppable, brokering deals that built my career and my life. But in 2008, the wave crashed, taking my job, marriage, and the home I'd once called my own. The financial crisis wasn't just a headline for me—it was a personal reckoning. Divorced, let go by the bank, and ultimately rather ironically foreclosed on by my lender, I stood amid the rubble of a life I'd carefully constructed. This chapter tells the story of how I turned the triggers of that collapse—loss, shame, guilt, and uncertainty—into truths that forged a new beginning.

My Picture-Perfect Life

Before the crisis, my world was one of spreadsheets, negotiating deals, and optimism. I thrived in the fast-paced environment of real estate finance, my days filled with loan approvals, meetings, and client handshakes. At home, in suburban southern California, we had the "picture-perfect" life. A new home, two cars, three amazing children, and the best German Shepard ever, Tyra. All a symbol of my success and hard work. But as the market teetered, so did my marriage. I clung to the belief that hard work could hold it all together. Then came the layoffs, the divorce papers, and the foreclosure notice—a trifecta of failure that left me reeling.

The triggers were everywhere: the "For Sale" sign on the lawn, the empty bedrooms, the silence where the family's laughter once rang. As a man who'd once measured success in deals closed and square footage financed, I found myself unmoored. My pastor, Jeff, offered the first lifeline, a simple yet profound analogy over one beautiful southern California morning: "Matt, sometimes no matter how hard you try, how many times you apologize or even the changes you make, you just can't fix everything. You might just have to start over with a whole new creation." Those words stuck a quiet challenge amid the chaos.

This chapter follows my journey from the depths of 2008 to my reinvention as a lawyer and a coach—not of high finance, but of divorce, a field I entered with the empathy of someone who'd lived its pain. It's the story of a man who learned to shake up the ruins of his past, transforming triggers into truths of resilience, purpose, and grace. From banker to broken to builder of a new life, my path offers a testament: even when the slate is wiped clean against your will, you can create something wonderfully new.

The Breaking Point

The day the foreclosure notice arrived, I felt the last thread of my old life snap. It was mid-2010; I stood in the driveway, the bank's letter crumpled in my fist, staring at the home I'd once financed with pride. The irony was suffocating: a real estate banker, master of loans, now locked out by the same system I'd fueled. Just months earlier, I lost my job at the bank as the financial crisis gutted the industry. Months before that, my wife and I had divorced, her stuff packed with a finality I couldn't negotiate away. The house was the last domino to fall, and any illusion of control went with it.

Let's go back just a bit. My unraveling had started with the whispers of trouble in the real estate market. By 2007, the cracks in the housing bubble were widening, but I kept pushing—closing deals, reassuring clients, staying late to crunch numbers. I am sure the stress seeped into our marriage. I was grinding away long days at work and commuting 2 to 4 hours every day. I knew things weren't great in our marriage, but I thought I was doing the right thing by working even harder in my career. Unfortunately, the divorce came during the financial crisis of 2008 and little did I know that was just the beginning of my personal crisis.

I was faking it well from 2008 to 2010. I was recently divorced but still a VP at the bank and living in my home. I had my kids half the time. I even coached my boys in the Little League and taught Sunday school at the church. You know the saying, "Fake it until you make it?" Well, I was the grand master of that statement. I made it look like everything was great in my life, yet underneath, I was a mess.

In 2010, the triggers piled up, such as delinquency notices and bills. The bank laid me off. Driving past the bank's gleaming tower sparked a flush of shame—how had I not seen it coming? Then, at home, the empty living room, stripped of family photos, echoed with regret—why hadn't I focused harder on the marriage? Even the mailbox, once a source of bills I could pay and offers for more credit, now mocked me with its final eviction notice. I tried to outrun it on my hikes in the hills around my neighborhood, but the fog only grew and surrounded me.

The New Picture

I remember my pastor, Jeff; he broke through the haze. We met at his office in one of those recently constructed buildings in the growing inland empire of southern California. I spilled it all—the job, divorce, the house—my voice finally cracking under the strain. Jeff listened, then leaned forward with a faint smile and gave me the Etch A Sketch theory. "Matt, do you remember the Etch A Sketch? Well, remember when you created a really cool picture on the Etch A Sketch and someone bumped into it and ruined the picture? Sometimes, no matter how hard you try, or how many changes you make, you just can't fix that picture. Well, sometimes life is just like that. Either you can choose to shake it up and start over or be stubborn and God will shake it up for you. Regardless, you *get to start it all over.*" I remember just staring at him, the words landing like a jolt. My life—my "perfect picture life"—had been bumped hard. No amount of work could restore it.

That night, alone in the house I'd soon leave, I sat on the bare floor, the pastor's metaphor echoing. The triggers weren't just losses—they were signals. The shame of the layoff pointed to the truth: my worth wasn't my job. The pain of the divorce revealed another truth: I'd neglected what mattered most. The foreclosure, a final blow, whispered freedom: I could start over. I definitely couldn't fix the old picture, but I could shake it up. The breaking point wasn't the end—it was the shake, the moment I decided to draw anew.

I would love to tell you some fantastic redemption "happily ever after" story, but like constructing a new building, the hard work was still ahead of me. I didn't have any blueprints to follow. I only knew that I had to get better, feel better, and be better. Be better: a better dad, a better friend, a better son, a better brother… really a better man. So, I started looking in every direction for a plan to follow, a class to take, a group to join, a book to study, a coach to train me, and anything to help me figure things out. I read more books, went to many groups, tried traditional counseling, watched more podcasts, and even started attending massive life-shifting events by Tony Robbins and hired one of his master coaches. In fact, I hired several coaches over the next 5 years. YES, IT TOOK ME FIVE YEARS to truly recover from this crisis. And, if I am totally honest, I still get triggered. But it is extremely different when I get triggered today. I don't spin completely out of control and barely even react now.

Honestly, I was always a trigger, walking around waiting to be pulled. Someone just cut me off in traffic, Triggered. Someone driving slow in the "fast" lane Triggered. See a happy family at the park, Triggered. Need a new tire on the car, Triggered. No money in the bank account, Triggered. Loan not approved, Triggered. Deal not closed, Triggered! See a failed marriage, Triggered.

Most people who know me post-recovery will probably not believe this story. I remember one particular instance of being triggered. I was driving, and this young guy cut me off so badly that I almost crashed. The trigger was pulled, and I was in pursuit of this inconsiderate a-hole. We aggressively sped through a pretty urban area near the beach, and at every stop sign, I tried to jump out of my car, and he would take off. Finally, I blew the next stop sign, pinned his car against the curb with my car, and confronted this guy and his friend. He pulled out a knife, and I proceeded to tell him that I was going to shove that up his, you know what. Well, thank goodness, someone yelled down that they were calling the police, and we both took off. Imagine what different outcomes could have been if he had pulled out a gun or even if I did beat these guys up; so what??? I would have probably gone to jail.

Later, I would think, what was the truth of this situation? This guy was a total jerk, sure. I was also driving like a total jerk. I was always in a hurry, impatient, and only really worried about where I was going. Hmmm, maybe that selfishness had something to do with my marriage not working out. Something to think about. The other truth was that I am a father to 3 amazing kids, and they deserve to have their dad around. This was reckless behavior that had to stop. The truth was that if I wasn't so unsteady, the beginning of this instance should have just scared me and not caused me to lose it.

The real truth revealed by digging into all of this was even deeper. As a father, I was there for my kids and their activities but never really present. I would show up at sporting and school events and still be glued to my phone. The truth is that I was showing up to be seen as "there" for my kids. The real truth is that my kids needed and deserved my full attention and presence if I was going to be there for them. A new picture of me was starting to take shape.

As I examined my life, I realized that I became a lawyer because my family said I should be a lawyer ever since I could remember. I guess it was because I was always negotiating. When I went to law school, I had very little plan or purpose for going to law school except for some things that I made up: Lawyers are successful, Lawyers are respected, Lawyers are smart, Lawyers have money and nice things. Then, I graduated from law school, passed the bar exam, passed another bar exam in another state, and finally realized I hated practicing law. Oh, and I wasn't making enough money to support our family. I was still bartending on weekends to have enough money. This wasn't worth it! So, I quit and entered the business world, ultimately leading me to the bank.

Let's get back to 2010. I shook myself off and started my real estate brokerage. If you can recall, 2010 probably wasn't the most ideal time to start a new business in the real estate market. It was a struggle to get started, for sure. So, the irony of all ironies happened: a friend asked me for help at her law practice, a DIVORCE LAW practice... ugh! Well, I needed a steady paycheck, so I said yes. Plus, I can do this while still building my real estate business.

Mind you, I am still in the middle of my crisis, and now I am getting triggered every day by people getting divorced and all of their stories. As my search for truth continued, I started asking better questions of myself.

Who Am I? Am I Matt, the Banker? Matt, the Real Estate Broker? Matt, the Dad? Matt, the Divorce Attorney? Matt, the Husband? Matt, the fun brother or friend? Is this just the typical mid-life or existential crisis? As I filled in the blanks a new creation is starting to emerge from the ashes of this crisis.

During this time of reconstruction, I had multiple breakthroughs and many breakdowns. Yet I found support in every project if I just looked for it. The random guy in a men's group would say something that hit me perfectly and made sense. Then, a divorce client would do something horrible to their former spouse, and I would find great appreciation for my former wife, who was the best mother for our children I could have ever hoped for and a great partner in co-parenting. I would get inspired by being on a mission trip in Mexico and seeing people living in poverty, yet they are very happy. I was finding truths in every turn of the knobs on my new Etch a Sketch. Some truths were painful; others were joyous, and all were ultimately beautiful.

Then, one day at the law office, I was sent to court on a case. I really hated going to court. Well, my client that day was this lovely woman, I'll call her "Jan." She was very sweet, and she told me a horrific story of abuse and neglect from her soon-to-be ex-husband. I was triggered; in fact, I thought to forget the court date; maybe I should just take this guy out in the parking lot. (I was still transforming some of these triggers into truths) Thankfully, I didn't do that. However, when we went into court that day, I was inspired to help tell Jan's truth, and, as they say, "the truth shall set you free." We "won" that day, but I am here to tell you there is no "winning" in divorce courts. There's just less loss.

The beauty of that day in court was not the "win." You see, after court, Jan was in shambles. She had no idea what she was going to do now. Her divorce was final. Yet, she was terrified of what was next. You see, she had just lost the last bit of certainty left in her life. Sure, she would be getting spousal support, and the kids were grown, but she didn't have any idea what was next. She and I would spend the rest of the afternoon in the parking lot. I was sweating in my suit but preaching like Pastor Jeff. I told her she now gets the opportunity to make a new picture on her Etch A Sketch, too. We laughed, cried, and even started drawing that picture of her new life creation. We even gave her a new name. Jan, the Bold and Beautiful experienced woman, would never ever let another man treat her like that again. Later, we refined that to Jan, the Bold and Beautiful: she would never let another human treat her like that again.

After that meeting, I was on such a natural high that I almost lost control of myself. I called my new partner, Renee, and was bouncing off the walls of my Nissan Maxima. I know what I am going to do: I am going to become a divorce coach! Of course, Renee said I was a glutton for punishment. I disliked being a divorce lawyer; I hated divorce, and I really didn't like how most people acted during their divorce. But, you see, my creation was starting to take shape. So, with absolute certainty and confidence, I said you see, I am going to be Saving Relationships One Divorce at a Time. She was like, wait, you are going to be a marriage recovery coach. I said, no, the marriage is done, over, and I am not trying to save that relationship. I am going to be a divorce recovery coach. I will help individuals transform the triggers of their divorces into the truths about themselves, their past, and their future amazing creations of themselves.

If I am honest, it didn't come out that clear on that day exactly. It took me a few years and countless trials and errors in my own life, and with many clients, most of them volunteered until that clear picture really emerged. Now that I have been doing this for almost 10 years, I have refined a process of Transforming those Triggers to Truth so that my clients find genuine happiness and levels of peace and joy they never imagined after their divorce. Most find that in the first few weeks of working with me, they have more peace than they have experienced in years. I believe that peace is the most powerful state of being. From that place of peace, we can shake up Etch A Sketch and start creating the most inspiring picture of their new future. This is the breath of life that lets them have a 2nd life, or for many of my clients, their 1st real relationship of love and respect with the most important intimate partner of their life… THEMSELVES.

\*\*\*

Contact:
www.freedominrelationships.com
www.facebook.com/freedominrelationshipscoaching
www.instagram.com/coachmatto
www.linkedin.com/in/matt-orzech-6647016

# Bethany Stone

Resilience is forged in the fires of adversity, and my journey reflects that truth. As the daughter of Swiss parents, I grew up surrounded by family and culture, and I aimed for a stable life through education and hard work. I graduated high school early, earned my teaching certification, and began my internship at seventeen. Despite a modest upbringing, I gained invaluable wisdom through experience.

At nineteen, I married. Ten years and three little boys later, I left that marriage with the impact of battered wife syndrome. I soon found myself in a more toxic relationship that preyed upon my fears and insecurities.

Through these challenges, I discovered my strength and embraced a growth mindset. This journey led me to seek peace, love, forgiveness, and joy. I reconnected with my passions, healing my heart, mind, and soul, and rediscovering myself. Today, as a speaker, author, mindset coach, and educator, I empower others to conquer fear and doubt. I share my story to help transform trials into triumphs, guiding others on their paths to true happiness.

# The Lesson of The Lollipop

## *By Bethany Stone*

The way we view our experiences is truly fascinating; two people, or even a lot of people, can go through the same events and emerge with completely different perspectives. These are my experiences and how my changing viewpoint transformed my life. Childhood experiences shape our outlook, since we first inherit the perspectives around us. My childhood was no different.

I grew up in a town with a population of one thousand—a small farming community in Idaho. We worked hard and our success was at the mercy of the weather's natural consequences on the crops. My mother was the daughter of a Swiss native, and my father was a newcomer to America who had just arrived from Switzerland. As a result, my home was rich in Swiss culture, encompassing both its positives and negatives. My siblings and I learned the values of strong work ethic, dedication, perseverance, determination, and plain old grit.

We were a musical family. We would wear traditional Swiss costumes as children and sing while my mom played the piano. We didn't have much money, but we had each other and the drive to better each situation we were in.

I was three when my parents learned I was an independent soul, not one to be pinned down. One day, while at home, my mom showed me a lollipop she would give me if I behaved. I don't remember why, but being my mischievous self, I didn't get the lollipop and felt wronged at such a deep level that I decided I would get one from the store myself. I rushed to my room, gathered my silver coins, found my little red tricycle, and rode to the gas station. We lived off a busy highway. I knew enough to ride on the side of the road. I remember being scared as semi-trucks whizzed by, and I recall my young mind's determination to reach that gas station.

When I arrived at the store, I parked my tricycle. I had made it, and I knew exactly where the lollipops were inside. After I'd selected my lollipop, a man waiting in the checkout behind me recognized me—small town benefits—and asked me how I got there. I told him

I rode my tricycle. He then put my tricycle in the back of his truck and drove me home. I didn't really care much at the time because, with my lollipop in hand, I claimed victory. Needless to say, on my return, my mom was shocked, worried, and mad. I didn't get to keep that lollipop.

As an adult, I relate to my mother's feelings. If my child rode off alone, I would've felt the same feelings of worry and would've enacted the same consequence. But for my childhood self, this small event shaped my lifelong view of the world and myself. I lived that experience. It was empowering. I felt victorious. I felt like I had solved the biggest problem ever!

Today, when my mom and I talk about it, you can still hear the frustration in her voice that I would've done that! And I agree. But from my three-year-old perspective, this strengthened my belief in myself and what I'm capable of. And though I am grown, I still feel a sense of pride and admiration in myself when I think of this event in my life. No moment is wasted, even when they seem like mistakes. This perspective, which I developed in childhood, laid the foundation for further shifts in my outlook and helped shape my future.

Another perspective story I've reflected on over the years was when my house burned down. I was sixteen. We lost not only our treasured possessions inside the house, but the entire structure also turned into ash as it burned to the ground, only leaving our roof in the wreckage. The memory of my house burning holds many emotions and feelings for me.

I wasn't there when my house caught fire; I was attending a national ballroom dance competition. My two older siblings were also away—one at college and the other on a church mission. As I competed, the people I knew wore too-sad looks and I -feel-bad-for-you gazes. Something felt wrong. They knew but waited to share the news until after the finals. After my partner and I placed second, my uncle walked across the dance floor, gave me a hug, and told me there'd been a fire at my house and my home burned down.

I returned to my hometown the next day. My family was staying at my Swiss grandmother's home in town. My whole family was in a state of shock. I heard my siblings' and my parents' rendition of where they were and what they experienced.

My home burned down during a terrible snowstorm. The ruthless temperatures and wind shut down roads and highways. Snow blocked our towns' volunteer fire department miles from their fire trucks. An electrical fire had started within the walls, as our home was over one hundred years old and not everything was updated. My brother awoke to smoke filling his room, then he woke everyone up. All my family members, except our poor dog, escaped the burning home.

At our grandmother's home, my family's physical belongings were gone; they didn't have toothbrushes, underwear, or clothing. I had more than any of my family members because I had a bag of dance clothing and things I'd packed for my ballroom competition. The nearest town was far away with only a Walmart.

Considering this, our small town pulled together, and every religious denomination donated to my family's immediate needs. My friends ransacked their dressers and gifted me their best school clothes. The tragedy of losing my home became a humbling time in my life. I gained perspective that the most treasured possessions I have are my family and friends—not the things I lost in the fire. This realization was the first mindset shift I experienced in this tragedy.

The second perspective shift happened within a couple of weeks of my house burning. I was supposed to compete in a scholarship program, but my dress—the one my mother sewed for weeks—for the poise and appearance category had burned up. And I also had nothing to wear for my dancing and vocal talent. Despite this, my friends urged me to compete anyway.

The next morning, outside of my grandmother's door, an envelope sat on the porch with my name on it. Inside, I found four hundred dollars and a note that read, *go get a dress.* Fairy Godmother's do exist.

With the money, my mom and I bought the most beautiful dress–hot pink with heavy beading on the bodice and a layered tulle skirt. I truly was Cinderella, just in pink, not blue. After throwing together a talent and gathering the rest of my wardrobe for the competition from family and friends, the day of the scholarship program came.

In the afternoon, judges conducted the interview portion of the competition. I'd done mock interviews to practice for this, and knew the judges expected confident, clear answers to their questions. I was called to go in first. I wasn't nervous. I don't get nervous very often—a little superpower I'd gained from my lollipop experience.

The girls around me smiled, saying, "Good luck," or "You got this." I was feeling good. Once in the room, I introduced myself and sat down at the long table. I was ready. Four judges sat in chairs across the table from me. A nice-looking lady asked, in what I heard as an overly sweet, pleasing voice, "What does your room look like right now?"

Ice cold dread replaced my confidence. What a shock to my soul! My mind flashed to the image of my roof lying on the rubble of our home,

My room was ash.

I'd thought I was handling losing my home well, but the strength I built up inside came crashing down. I couldn't respond. Instead, I started to cry. I'll never forget the shock on the judges' faces. I wasn't politely crying either; I was full-on-ugly crying, with noises, sniffling, uncontrollable tears, and an inability to utter coherent words. I vaulted to my feet, knowing I wasn't going to pull myself together, and fled the room. This wasn't a fairytale; I left no glass slipper behind. It wouldn't matter what dress I wore now—I'd ruined my chances in the competition and let everyone down.

Pure fear terrorized the other girls' faces as I left that room. One by one, they approached the door to their judges' interview without knowing the context of my tears. Later, when the competitors were backstage, the other girls shared with me that my tears shook their confidence before their interviews. We were in the same situation, competing for scholarship money and going through this interview process together.

I like using this example when teaching about perspective, because there are multiple perspectives to consider. My friends didn't cry in their interviews though the judges asked that same question to more than one girl. But my reaction to that question differed because of what I recently lived through. I thought I was okay, but my perspective shifted. My experience made it impossible to function when others could. I wasn't okay; I was traumatized, and despite my confidence and preparation, I couldn't control my tears. My trauma changed the outcome of a successful interview, costing me potential scholarship money. If you asked me today, "What does your room look like right now?" I wouldn't react as I did when I was sixteen and traumatized. I'd respond in a comparable way to my friends that day. But at sixteen, because of circumstances my perspective differed.

From this story I learned, our emotional well-being and awareness of those emotions tie directly to our environment and our immediate situations. These two forces, environment and situation, often play a crucial role in how we behave, how we feel and how we treat others. Because of this, I argue that happiness is *supposed* to ebb and flow. The trauma of my house burning brought about heartache—I was not okay—and the question the judge posed increased my awareness of that heartache—I *knew* I was not okay. In order to understand the positive emotions, we crave, we need to go through difficult situations that bring about hard emotions and poke at our awareness of those emotions. Then we know where we are at, without denial ,and we have a place to start.

One final emotional awareness change I underwent came from the choices of others, which often can be more dangerous and more damaging than fire. I ended a troubled marriage of ten years. We had three little boys. My ex-husband was a good man but had too many personal demons to conquer, and as a result, his behavior was damaging to my boys and I.

I left that marriage diagnosed with battered wife syndrome. Because I was in such a state of disarray, a truly abusive person preyed upon my weakness. He sought me out, told me lies, and when I questioned anything, he claimed I couldn't see things his way because of my ex. The cloud of low self-esteem and fear pushed me into denial of what was really happening to that lollipop driven girl I once was—I was losing myself. This man convinced me to marry him, knowing I was in a fragile state, within months of meeting him.

I now have discovered my first husband had demons in his life because of substances that stole his will. In contrast, my second husband was intentionally abusive rather than unintentionally reacting and lashing out because of addiction. He put me through pain purposefully. He controlled me and gas lit me, constantly blaming his lack of success in his job, his children's outbursts, his health issues—all of it—on me, my past, or my children. We were the cause of everything wrong in his life. He forced me to quit my job. He controlled our money, and he demanded to go with me everywhere I went. His physiological abuse drove me to thoughts of suicide for the first time in my life, and I planned it. But even in this, miraculously my perspective saved me.

When I was at my lowest, too sad to get out of bed and thinking about the pills I could take to make the pain go away, I looked out my window. Right there, on a branch, was a hummingbird couple making their little nest.

Hummingbird nests are usually difficult to see. The birds build flexible nests with spider silks, cotton, mosses, and other soft materials they find, intricately shaping them with their bodies. As I lay in bed watching this little miracle happen, hope started to grow within me–a little bit of that victorious lollipop-loving child shone through. And, like I did at sixteen, I realized what I felt—I felt lost. But if I was only lost, I could be found again. From then on, I became like those birds and began building myself back up.

I started to write. I'd stopped because my husband mocked me for writing and used my embarrassment against me. But that couldn't matter now. Through writing I connected with my feelings and attached me to *me* again. In words on a page, I saw where I was losing myself and started to pick up those pieces. I started to cook again. I started to run, dance and exercise. I started calling my family and friends again. However, starting to find myself also started causing some ripples in my abusive marriage, especially when I began standing up for myself.

Pushing back against my newfound hope, he became more abusive, so much so, his abuse escalated into physically assaulting me while I was putting on makeup. Afterwards, he told me that he acted out of self-defense because I had a blush brush in my hand. He called the police officers to remove me from the house. He worked in law and would manipulate it for his benefit. When the police officers came, he told them he felt threatened by me. I never threatened him, never touched him. I was the one covered in bruises.

One police officer took me aside, told me I was being physically and emotionally abused. Because I built myself into more of myself again, denial couldn't reach me as easily. When I heard the police officer's words, I knew they were true. He advised me to get out now, asked if I had family nearby, and informed me he was going to sight my husband and prevent him from entering the house for eight hours. He gave me a card for the victims' advocates in town and urged me to contact them.

I called my parents, a couple of siblings—the people I valued more than those things turned to ash or any item we packed—and they had me and my boys moved out in less than three hours.

Since this happened, I've never spoken with my ex-husband again. We saw each other at the mediation to sign the divorce papers, but because of my journey back to myself and standing up for myself, he knows that I will not be controlled. *I'll not be pinned down.*

We all experience moments when we wish to transform and change our emotional or physical state, and while this isn't a simple thing to do, it's essential. Once you see what you want to change, when perspective shifts then start there. Start from where you are at. Begin with that hope.

From this experience I learned that our perspective and our desire for change are connected, each strengthening the other. As you add small changes, your perspective will fuel further transformation and further desire to change, causing a snowball effect. Start with small changes in your situation and your environment. As I learned from my second perspective shift when my house burned down, your environment directly ties to your feelings. By altering your environment, you alter how you feel. Change up or establish routines, friendships, diet, what you listen to, watch, and read. By continually moving forward, even if you are not perfect at doing so, you gradually build the emotional and physical self you want, piece by piece.

My life now resembles what I thought could only happen in fairy tales. I have an amazing husband who supports and encourages me and loves my boys. When we met, my traumatized perspective was that every man is inherently evil. I had the history to prove that thought pattern. He was very persistent and worked hard on having me agree to that first date. Once again, my perspective shifted.

All these stories I have shared contain my truth. I have learned on a deep level that when you open yourself up to happiness, knowing that life won't be roses and sunshine, you open yourself up to love, forgiveness, peace, and a life you could only dream of. Is my life perfect? Far from it. But I do feel content with where I am and possess an infinite sense of gratitude for the experiences that have shaped me and taught me how to be who I am today.

I still have that hummingbird nest to this day. I took it from the tree after the little ones had left. It reminds me that I want to ensure my perspective supports the same drive I had when I was three years old riding my tricycle. My perspective of knowing what I want—whatever that lollipop is—and working until I feel the satisfaction of victory in my gasp. My story may help you. Allow perspective shifts to change the way you look at things. Find hope in even the tiniest glimmers, because what you tell yourself today can change your perspective for tomorrow.

***

Bethany Stone,

Mindset and Life Skills Coach, Speaker, Author, and Educator

Website: www.thrivingbynature.com

Email: Bethany@thrivingbynature.com

Social:

https://www.instagram.com/thriving_by_nature_coaching/#

https://www.facebook.com/profile.php?id=61562381904802

# Renee (Vee) Vardouniotis

Renee (Vee) Vardouniotis is a Speech-Language Pathologist, Mindset and Communication Specialist, Conference Host, and Founder of The Edge Academy. With a passion for empowering young minds, Renee works with individuals to develop self-belief, resilience, and a competitive edge in academics, sports, business, and life. She believes confidence isn't just a feeling—it's a skill that can be developed with the right mindset and tools.

With years of experience providing Speech Therapy, Renee has seen firsthand how communication and self-belief are deeply connected. She goes beyond traditional therapy, blending mindset coaching with practical strategies to help individuals overcome self-doubt, express themselves clearly, and embrace a growth mindset. Through The Edge Academy, she partners with schools, parents, and organizations to deliver engaging group coaching, hands-on workshops, and inspiring speaking engagements.

As a mother of two, Renee understands the pressures today's teens face—from academic stress, to self-doubt, to social expectations. She's passionate about creating spaces where young adults feel seen, heard, and capable of greatness. Her approach is real, relatable, and results-driven, giving young adults the tools to show up fully in every aspect of life—whether in the classroom, on the field, or in personal relationships.

Renee's vision is to build environments and cultivate communities where confidence is nurtured, self-belief is reinforced, and every person feels empowered to succeed.

# Think and Grow Confident

## *By Renee Vee*

Much of the inspiration for this chapter comes from my first mentor, Bob Proctor—a self-help guru and prosperity teacher who dedicated over 60 years to uncovering the transformative principles in Napoleon Hill's classic, *Think and Grow Rich*. Hill studied the habits and mindsets of 500 of the top 1% of performers, offering us a timeless blueprint for success and fulfillment. Bob shared this invaluable knowledge with me, raising my awareness of the incredible power we all possess within. Now, I have the privilege and honor of passing these teachings on to you.

To **Think and Grow Confident** means to go beyond merely seeking wealth and instead build a life overflowing with purpose, passion, resilience, and fulfillment. It implies that by cultivating positive, powerful thoughts and a strong, resilient mindset, a person can grow their capacity to face challenges and develop inner strength, or "might". This idea is rooted in the notion that our thoughts shape our reality. If we think confidently and with purpose, we are more likely to take the actions that lead to growth and success, both mentally and in tangible outcomes. It's a reminder that greatness begins in the mind and grows outward from there.

By embracing and practicing the following concepts, you will empower yourself to achieve greatness in every area of your life. As you learn to develop a powerful mindset, you'll realize your potential for extraordinary success—financial, emotional, and spiritual.

**It's important to note that knowledge alone does not create change.**

Raising your awareness to these concepts is only the first step. You may have heard many of these ideas before, perhaps in books, seminars, or even from well-meaning friends. However, without making the decision to practice them, they remain little more than vocabulary in your mental dictionary. The magic happens only when you decide to **live** these principles. True transformation comes when you take **consistent action** and integrate what you learn into your daily life. Personal development is a lifelong process, one that requires **commitment, practice, and growth** over time. Simply reading and understanding isn't enough. It's the **DOING**—and the dedication to ongoing improvement—that brings real, lasting change.

The first concept is intentionally placed at the beginning because, without it, we cannot fully become the best version of ourselves. Without it, true success remains out of reach. I am not sure why we live in a world that paints self-love as selfish, when it is absolutely essential for a healthy, balanced life. Teaching our kids self-love is crucial to breaking generational patterns of self-doubt and low self-worth. We can't give our children what we don't have, so remember; self-love in your kids begins with YOU. When you practice self-respect, self-compassion, and confidence in yourself, you set a powerful example for them to follow. Teaching them to love themselves starts with how you love and value yourself.

## SELF-LOVE – Know That You Are Flaw-some

If I asked you to list five things that you love, would "ME" be on that list?

## YOU SHOULD BE #1 ON THAT LIST.

Yes. Before family, before kids, before pets, before ANYTHING. Why? Because we can't fully love anything if we don't love ourselves. It is the foundation for a fulfilling life, making us better parents, friends, partners, and professionals. Self-love isn't just about feeling good; it enables us to give our best to the people and world we care about.

It's easy to get caught in the whirlwind of external pressures and forget about the importance of internal nurturing. When we prioritize ourselves—our well-being, our mental health, and our growth—everything else falls into place. Without self-love, we can become disconnected from our true desires and needs, leaving us feeling unfulfilled and disconnected from the world around us. But when we practice self-love, we can live from a place of inner strength and peace, no matter what external challenges we may face.

**Want to improve your mental wellness?**

LOVE YOURSELF.

Loving yourself helps develop a positive self-image, reducing the risk of depression, anxiety, and other mental health challenges. It cultivates inner peace and resilience, allowing you to face stress and adversity with greater ease. Without a strong sense of self-love, even the smallest setbacks can feel overwhelming. But when you love yourself, you approach life's obstacles as opportunities for growth rather than insurmountable challenges.

**Want to improve your emotional intelligence?**

LOVE YOURSELF.

Daily self-compassion creates emotional stability and resilience, helping you through tough times without excessive self-criticism or negative self-talk. The more you practice self-love, the more connected you become to your emotional landscape. This awareness enables you to regulate your emotions more effectively, leading to healthier responses to stress, conflict, and disappointment.

**Want healthy relationships?**

LOVE YOURSELF.

When we love ourselves, we set boundaries, communicate our needs clearly, and respect both ourselves and others. This enables us to give and receive love genuinely, cultivating relationships based on mutual respect and understanding. Healthy relationships are built on a foundation of self-worth—if you don't value yourself, you will struggle to create relationships that reflect that value. Love is not a transaction; it's a reflection of who we are. When we are centered in self-love, we are better able to attract relationships that are equally enriching for everyone involved.

**Want to be happier every day?**

LOVE YOURSELF.

Self-acceptance allows us to embrace our true selves—flaws and all. It encourages authenticity, freeing us from the need to seek external validation or approval. True happiness comes from within. When you love yourself unconditionally, you become free from the traps of comparison, jealousy, and the need to "measure up" to others' standards. You create your own definition of success and happiness, one that is deeply rooted in self-respect and self-acceptance.

**Want to make others' lives better?**

LOVE YOURSELF.

When we practice self-love, we take control of our lives and make decisions that align with our values. Our self-respect and confidence inspire those around us to do the same, creating a ripple effect that promotes a culture of positivity and self-care. By becoming the best version of ourselves, we inspire others to do the same. Our actions speak louder than words—when you show up fully as your authentic self, others will feel empowered to do the same.

## THOUGHT POWER – Your Mind is a Garden

The power of our thoughts is immense. They shape our perceptions, influence our emotions, and ultimately dictate our actions. Each thought has the potential to mold our reality, either positively or negatively. By choosing which thoughts we allow to remain in our minds, we can steer our lives in the direction we desire. The more we understand how our thoughts create our reality, the more we can take control over them to design a life that serves our highest good.

Consider the ripple effect of a single thought. A negative thought can breed doubt, fear, and limitation, chaining us to a cycle of self-sabotage. Conversely, a positive thought can ignite hope, confidence, and ambition, propelling us toward growth and fulfillment.

**Our minds are like gardens**—the seeds we plant determine what grows. If we plant seeds of doubt, negativity, or fear, we'll harvest more of those things in our lives. If we plant seeds of positivity, gratitude, and possibility, we will experience more of the same. It is so important to be mindful of what we allow to take root in our minds.

We have the power to choose our thoughts. By being aware and practicing mindfulness, we can observe our thoughts without judgment and intentionally direct our focus toward those that serve our highest good. When you cultivate the ability to observe your thoughts, you give yourself the freedom to choose which ones you engage with and which ones you dismiss.

Our thoughts also possess a vibrational energy that resonates with the universe, attracting events and circumstances that match our inner state. This is the foundation of the Law of Attraction. When you are filled with positive, high-vibration thoughts, you attract opportunities, people, and experiences that reflect that energy. The universe is always responding to your energy—it's like a mirror that reflects whatever you project.

Through practices like visualization, affirmation, and gratitude, we can channel the transformative power of our thoughts to manifest our dreams and create the life we envision. By mastering our thoughts, we realize our true potential and experience profound fulfillment in every aspect of our lives. Start by taking a moment each day to visualize your ideal life. Close your eyes, see yourself in the scenario you desire, and feel the emotions associated with it. The more vividly you imagine your success, the more your thoughts will align with your desired outcome.

## CONFIDENCE – Meet Your Secret Superpower

Confidence is the belief in our abilities and judgment, and it's a powerful trait that influences every aspect of our lives. It empowers us to face challenges and pursue our goals with determination. Confidence isn't about arrogance—it's about a quiet, unwavering belief in yourself, even when others may doubt you. It's the courage to stand tall in the face of adversity and pursue your passions without hesitation.

Building confidence is a journey that requires self-awareness, practice, and resilience. It's a muscle that gets stronger the more you use it. And while confidence doesn't come overnight, small wins each day compound to create a foundation that can carry you through even the toughest challenges.

Confidence is not about being perfect—it's about trusting yourself to handle whatever comes your way. It helps you perform better, make decisions with clarity, and maintain a positive outlook even in adversity. Even when things don't go according to plan, confident people tend to bounce back quickly and keep going.

Confident people often seem like they have a certain vibe about them- it's as if they walk into a room and just know they belong there. Of course, even confident people have off days and areas that they struggle. If you are looking to increase your confidence, you can start by looking at these traits. Which ones do you see in yourself already? Which ones could you work on?

**7 Traits of a Confident Person:**

- **They take risks**

Confident people may be less afraid to step out of their comfort zone. They know that to grow, you must try new things, even if it means you might not succeed every time.

- **They're optimistic**

Confident people tend to be more positive and expect good things to happen. Even when things go wrong, they can see those experiences and even failures as a chance to learn and get better.

- **They accept compliments**

When someone says, "Hey, great job," a confident person has an easier time saying, "thank you," instead of shrugging it off. They're not bragging, they energetically receive compliments and know their worth.

- **They're decisive**

Confident people find it easier to make decisions and stick to them. They trust their instincts and don't waste time worrying about what everyone else may think.

- **They set boundaries**

Knowing when to say yes and when to say no is a sign of confidence. Confident people respect their own limits and aren't afraid to communicate them to others.

- **They're not pretenders**

Confident people are more comfortable being who they are and don't feel the need to pretend to be someone they're not.

- **They listen more than they speak**

Surprisingly, confident people often listen more than they talk. They're secure enough to know they don't always have to be the loudest voice in the room.

## DECISION MAKING – Be a Decision Ninja

There's a single mental action that can quickly resolve significant challenges and improve almost any business or personal scenario you face. This skill has the power to launch you toward extraordinary success. It's called **decision-making**. The ability to make decisions quickly and effectively is one of the key traits of high performers.

Proficient decision-makers often achieve substantial financial success, but the impact of their choices extends far beyond income alone. Decisions shape every aspect of life, from mental and physical well-being to social interactions and career trajectory. Good decisions are the building blocks of a well-lived life.

To become an excellent decision-maker, here are a few tips:

- **Clarity is key.**

When making decisions, it's crucial to have clarity about your values, goals, and the desired outcome. The more aligned your decision is with your true desires, the more confident you will feel in your choice.

- **Limit your options.**

Having too many choices can lead to decision paralysis. Narrow your options and focus on the ones that resonate most with your values and goals.

- **Trust your instincts.**

Gut feelings are often based on your subconscious knowledge, and they can be powerful guides when making decisions. Trusting your intuition can help you make decisions with greater speed and confidence.

- **Make decisions quickly and adjust later.**

Taking too long to make decisions often leads to missed opportunities. Make a choice, and if it doesn't work out, adjust as you go. The key is to stay flexible and keep moving forward.

## FAITH OVER FEAR – Take a Leap of Faith

Fear is a natural human emotion that exists for a reason: it helps keep us safe. But while fear has its purpose, it can also act as a barrier to growth and success. Fear of failure, fear of judgment, fear of the unknown—these fears can keep us stuck in our comfort zones and prevent us from seizing the opportunities that will elevate us.

The antidote to fear is **faith**—faith in yourself, your abilities, and the process of growth. When you choose to have faith over fear, you empower yourself to take bold steps and pursue your dreams with courage.

Fear can distort our perception of reality, amplifying worst-case scenarios and paralyzing us from taking action. But when we lean into faith, we gain the confidence to move forward even in the face of uncertainty.

**How do you cultivate faith over fear?**

- **Shift your perspective.**

Fear often arises from focusing on potential negative outcomes. Shift your focus to the positive possibilities that lie ahead.

- **Embrace uncertainty.**

Life is inherently uncertain. The more you can accept uncertainty as part of the process, the less control fear will have over you.

- **Take small risks.**

The more you practice stepping out of your comfort zone, the more comfortable you become with uncertainty. Every small risk builds your confidence and faith in the process.

# EMOTIONAL INTELLIGENCE – Study Your Emotionomics

Emotional Intelligence (EQ) is the capacity to recognize, understand, and manage our emotions while also understanding and influencing the emotions of others. High EQ is critical for success in all areas of life, especially in leadership, communication, and relationships.

EQ consists of four core components:

**Self-awareness** – The ability to recognize and understand your emotions and how they influence your thoughts and behavior.

**Self-regulation** – The ability to manage your emotions and reactions, particularly in stressful or challenging situations.

**Social awareness** – The ability to empathize with others, understand their emotions, and navigate social dynamics effectively.

**Relationship management** – The ability to communicate clearly, build trust, and manage conflicts constructively.

Unlike IQ, which tends to be relatively stable, EQ can be improved over time with practice. It is always possible to become more empathetic, manage stress better, and enhance your communication skills. In developing your EQ, you will ultimately benefit from a greater ability to adapt and be resilient, which leads to better leadership, teamwork, and interpersonal relationships. Other benefits of high EQ: lower levels of stress and anxiety, better heart health, and stronger immune functioning.

While our formal education system currently emphasizes cognitive intelligence (IQ) as the main success indicator, studies suggest that EQ can be a better predictor of success than IQ. Our schools focus on measurable academic achievements like math, science, and reading, while largely overlooking emotional intelligence (EQ). This focus on IQ prioritizes skills that can be quantified through tests and assessments, rather than skills that are less tangible but equally crucial for personal and professional success.

The lack of emphasis on EQ in schools can lead to several challenges for our youth and adults alike. The first being underdeveloped social skills. Without a focus on EQ, students may struggle with skills like empathy, conflict resolution, and collaboration. These are critical for forming healthy relationships and succeeding in team environments, yet these skills are often not directly taught or nurtured in the classroom.

Another challenge is high stress levels. Academic pressure and the competitive nature of IQ

focused education can increase student stress. EQ skills, such as emotional regulation and self

compassion, can be protective factors against anxiety and burnout, yet students often don't

receive formal guidance on developing these tools.

Employers increasingly value "soft skills"—such as communication, empathy, and teamwork—which are all rooted in EQ. Graduates may be well-prepared technically, but without emotional intelligence, they can struggle with collaboration, leadership, and navigating workplace dynamics.

It seems our formal education system could benefit from a significant overhaul to meet the needs of today's world. It's funny, Napoleon Hill mentions similar thoughts in *Think and Grow Rich*, a book published in 1937! Makes you wonder, doesn't it?

## MY HOPE FOR YOU

Begin to develop and practice these concepts, and you will undoubtedly Think and Grow Confident. The journey to a mighty life starts with self-love—embrace who you are, flaws and all. Let go of limiting beliefs and tap into your power as the highest form of creation on this Earth. Cultivate emotional intelligence and confidence and be brave enough to make decisions that align with your dreams. Take leaps of faith, even in the face of fear, and trust that the universe will conspire in your favor. The world is waiting for your greatness.

You have everything it takes. Embrace the power within you. Believe in yourself. If you need to, you can always borrow my sincere belief in you. I am your biggest fan!

*\*\*\**

To contact Renee:

www.reneevee.com

www.linkedin.com/in/renee-vardouniotis

www.instagram.com/renee__vee

# Tonya Drummonds

Tonya Drummonds is a dedicated and inspiring Life Coach with a proven track record of guiding high-performing individuals to break their barriers and achieve extraordinary success. She combines compassion, powerful communication, and a talent for building deep, authentic relationships to create safe and transformative environments for clients. Tonya is a dual-certified coach who has learned several coaching disciplines to effectively empower clients to reach their full potential as their trusted partner. Tonya is based in Austin, Texas, and works with clients worldwide.

With over 26 years of experience as a cybersecurity leader in the tech industry, Tonya enjoyed a rewarding career prior to becoming a Life Coach. She led global teams of innovators, strategists, and security professionals. She excelled as a dynamic leader and contributed to many enterprise successes for the Fortune 500 company she was employed with.

Tonya is passionate about leadership mentoring and contributing to professional development organizations that educate, empower, and champion personal and professional growth. She enjoys speaking at conferences and various forums to share her story, expertise, and experiences and stay connected with thought leaders.

When she's not coaching, Tonya enjoys traveling, reading, learning new things, cooking with her husband, and entertaining friends and family. She's an avid fisherwoman (yes, she can catch fish like a pro).

# A Journey through Fear – A Destination of Freedom

## By Tonya Drummonds

Think of a moment when fear held you back. Perhaps it was the whisper of doubt before a big presentation, the tremor of anxiety before a tough conversation, or the paralyzing dread that stopped you from chasing a dream. We've all been there, trapped in the labyrinth of our own anxieties.

But what if there's a way out? What if those fears—those seemingly insurmountable obstacles—hold the keys to profound liberation? I invite you on a journey: a journey through fear to the destination of freedom.

Many would describe me as brave. What they don't see is the tightening in my chest, the racing thoughts of fainting in the moment, or the invisible wall that springs up between me and my desires. My fear, though a natural protector, often overstayed its welcome and became a cage. Let me explain.

I'm now a Life Coach, and I love it. Before making the leap to leave my corporate career, fear was my constant companion. I was a Director of Cybersecurity for a large, global Fortune 500 company. I was comfortable, enjoying the challenge of stretching myself and my team, performing at a high level, and learning new things. Life was good.

But I had fears—plenty of them: fear of stagnation and not reaching the next level, fear of speaking out against the favoritism I saw in executive management, fear of abandoning my team by leaving, and fear of leaping into the unknown, giving up a great job and salary to pursue what I truly wanted—to leave corporate life behind.

With those fears in tow, I hired a Life Coach who helped me unlock life-changing feelings of freedom. With her guidance, I began to dream of what I really wanted, why it mattered, and who I'd become if I could change careers without failing. Have you ever imagined what you'd do if failure weren't possible? That's mental freedom, and it's powerful. This wasn't a frivolous exercise—it was the catalyst for change.

I relished the mental freedom to explore, dream, and plan. I could see my future take shape and become achievable by mapping a path forward. Ironically, a layoff just three days after signing up for coach training cemented my freedom in life and career. After a few minutes of shock, I realized this unexpected change was a blessing. The severance from my long tenure provided the resources to launch my coaching career.

This experience taught me that while fear is a constant companion, freedom—when embraced—can reshape reality. True freedom lies in using it to create a life I truly desire.

That reminds me of a recent conversation with a friend. He shared his misery at work, revealing a pattern of fear he hadn't recognized. He recounted a demeaning comment from his executive about a vacation request, which left him deeply upset. When I asked why he hadn't spoken up, he cited "worry" about retaliation and job loss. I challenged him: "Why live in fear?" and "Why not seek new opportunities?" He initially denied living in fear, but when I replaced "worry" with "fear," the truth hit him—they're the same feeling. Visibly shaking off that realization, he smiled and committed to job hunting and speaking up in his next one-on-one with his leader. As we parted, his clarity and empowerment were palpable.

I encourage you to reflect on challenges you've faced in your career. Assess your feelings and reactions to them. If they're rooted in fear, know you have the power to change that.

- What would you pursue if failure were impossible?
- Is fear stopping you from dreaming boldly or exploring new possibilities?

We've explored how fear hinders potential in careers. What about life and relationships? Can you recall times when fear disrupted your success in those areas?

Earlier, I said fear is my constant companion. I've conquered some big fears, but the smaller ones linger—a lifelong challenge I must manage rather than eliminate. Why am I so sure? Fears can hide in perceived strengths.

I once proudly identified as an over-achiever, a trait I thought was admirable. I believed being ultra-driven was exceptional. But during a coaching session focused on my achievements, I admitted I wasn't as happy as I'd expected when reaching big goals. Disliking that realization, I wondered, "How could hitting my goals leave me hollow?" "Is that why I'd rush to the next achievement so quickly?"

In another session using Positive Intelligence®, I discovered my intense fear of failure had fixated me on destinations, neglecting the richness of the journey. I'd failed to celebrate relationships, support, learning, honored values, and personal growth. Wow.

Now, my life embraces the present—the right here and now. I savor each step, nurturing deep connections with loved ones. I feed my curiosity with weekly learning through books, mentorship, and others' stories. I "dance in the moment," extracting joy from every experience. I find clarity in nature, listening to birdsong and appreciating beauty. Gratitude flows for those who offer love and support. I've rekindled childhood friendships, sharing laughter and memories. This newfound appreciation brings profound happiness and fulfillment, even before reaching my goals.

Understanding my fear of failure shifted my perspective. Will it stay crystal clear forever? No, but I can recognize when I've slipped into hyper-drive and correct it faster. That's progress!

- What fear is your constant companion?
- Have you taken steps to manage it and shift your perspective?

It's likely sinking in now: fear can sharpen our thinking, but when it lingers, it breeds doubt, worry, or inaction. After exploring career and life fears, let's turn to relationships.

Do you know someone who consistently over-gives or prioritizes others' needs over their own? Someone who rarely shares opinions, avoids speaking up, and always defers to others, going along to get along? You might think they're easy-going—but are they?

I have a friend who's truly easy-going yet has opinions, stands up when needed, and sets boundaries to protect her happiness without over-giving. I can count on her anytime.

So, what fear drives the person who over-gives and stays silent? Often, it's fear of rejection.

A co-worker from my distant past once shared the heavy burden of not saying what she truly wanted to her family and friends. At work, she was different—able to speak up and protect her happiness. Intrigued, I asked about how her loved ones treated her. She mentioned something telling: her husband often asked, "Is that how you really feel?" when seeking her opinion. He couldn't trust her to give honest feedback. Yet, when he offered her constructive criticism and saw her expression shift, he'd soften his words to avoid hurting her. Her self-doubt was clear, and he constantly tried to bolster her with encouragement. She noticed other family members treated her similarly.

I asked, "What's the worst that could happen if you told your loved ones the truth?" "What if they appreciated it?" As she reflected, she realized she could bring the confidence she had at work into her personal life.

She chose to change the lose-lose dynamic with her family and friends. She couldn't offer or receive true support, missing out on the deep, healthy relationships she craved and deserved. She also saw how exhausting it must be for her loved ones to constantly reassure her of her worth. This self-awareness was pivotal in rebuilding her self-esteem and trustworthiness.

Later, she shared that this fear stemmed from childhood. She was shocked to find it still lingered as an adult, wife, and mother. She chose to break free from those early fears.

- Is fear of abandonment, intimacy, betrayal, or rejection affecting your relationships?
- Are childhood events shaping your relationships today?

Did you know fears can be inherited or learned? It's not just cheekbones, good looks, or hair (or lack thereof) we inherit. Beyond our own experiences, we can absorb fears from our families, passed down through generations via reactions, warnings, stories, and temperaments. This subtle transmission shapes our emotional landscape.

It's not hopeless, though. A brief, thorough look at childhood memories—what we heard from parents and family—can reveal fascinating ties to our present selves. Consider these three scenarios:

**Career Issues – Childhood Scenario:**

A child hears parents repeatedly say, "They don't value my work," "I'm always overlooked," or "It's pointless to ask; they'll just say no." They may grow up believing their efforts are unappreciated and they're powerless to change it. They might avoid asking for a raise, even when deserved, assuming it's futile. This fear intensifies if they struggle with low self-esteem at work, feeling unworthy of recognition or advancement.

**Financial Issues – Childhood Scenario:**

A child hears constant parental worry about money and the consequences of not getting a raise. They may enter adulthood believing there's never enough. They might not request a raise, fearing it could jeopardize job security and lead to financial ruin. They might undervalue their skills, accept low pay, and live with financial anxiety and a scarcity mindset.

**Relationship Issues – Childhood Scenario:**

A child hears, "Relationships are always hard," "People always let you down," "All men or women cheat," "Love is a lie," or "Relationships are a waste of time." They may develop a deep fear of emotional intimacy, struggling with vulnerability, avoiding closeness, or sabotaging healthy relationships with suspicion. They might not recognize traits like respect, trust, and communication, normalizing toxic behaviors and failing to set healthy boundaries.

**A Loving Note to Parents:**

Examine your fear-based or negative communication around your children. They're absorbing it all, and the cycle will persist unless you break it—a cycle that likely started with you.

As we near the end of this journey through fear toward freedom, I ask: Do you see the irony?

We yearn for liberation—to pursue dreams, express our authentic selves, and live unburdened by "what ifs." Yet, we often let fear—

of failure, rejection, judgment, or the unknown—dictate our choices and shrink our world.

Whether we admit it or not, experiences become ingrained narratives. We associate actions or situations with negative outcomes, building a mental fortress of "shouldn'ts" and "can'ts."

Concluding Reflection:

- How many opportunities have you missed because of fear?
- How many dreams remain unfulfilled, silenced by "what ifs"?

Don't be discouraged! True freedom isn't the absence of fear—it's the courage to act despite it. It's stepping beyond your comfort zone, embracing vulnerability, and choosing growth over stagnation. It's the exhilarating feeling of taking control of your narrative and writing your own story.

Freedom is found in:

- Challenging limiting beliefs—testing their accuracy
- Embracing vulnerability—being seen, imperfections and all
- Taking calculated risks—venturing beyond the norm
- Practicing self-compassion—being kind when we stumble
- Focusing on the present—letting go of past regrets and future worries

While concise, the list represents a challenging set of skills to master. Identify and request mature and trusted friends to render assistance. Find and engage the guidance of a Life Coach, like I did.

Remember that **the journey to freedom is not an outward expedition**, a quest for external circumstances that liberate you. **It's an inward voyage**, a descent into the depths of your own being, where your deepest fears reside. This chapter is an invitation to embark on that journey, to become intimate with the anxieties that shape your choices and limit your potential.

There will be stumbles, moments of doubt, and the temptation to retreat. But with each act of courage, you will reclaim a piece of yourself. You will expand your horizons, discover hidden strengths, and build a life that resonates with your deepest desires.

Are you ready? Take a deep breath… then step onto the road that leads you to true and lasting freedom.

***

LET'S CONNECT:

Email: tld@enhancedbycoaching.com

Website: www.enhancedbycoaching.com

LinkedIn: https://www.linkedin.com/in/tldrummonds/

Book a Free Discovery/

Breakthrough Session:

# Dahlya Brown Shook

Dahlya Brown Shook, MOT, CMHIMP, CHC, is a Trauma-Informed Mindfulness Specialist, Integrative Medicine Health Coach, and Reiki Master who transitioned from the traditional healthcare system to offer clients rapid, whole-body healing. With a Master's in Occupational Therapy, certifications in Integrative Medicine for Mental Health, Holistic Health Coaching, Somatics, Movement, and Energy Healing, and an extensive background in disease management, brain health, pediatrics, detoxification, and mental health, Dahlya blends clinical expertise with holistic healing to create radical transformations.

Her deep understanding of neuroscience, sensory processing, gut-brain optimization, and trauma regulation allows her to bridge the gap between science, medicine, and intuitive healing. She guides ambitious empaths, mindful leaders, and individuals of all ages from all walks of life through the process of rewiring their nervous systems, breaking free from chronic stress, and creating sustainable well-being.

Dahlya's philosophy is that true healing goes beyond symptom management—it requires addressing root causes, restoring internal safety, and rebalancing the body, mind, and spirit. By integrating evidence-based medical approaches with energy work and functional therapies, she empowers clients to transcend trauma, enhance self-trust, and cultivate lasting health and prosperity.

Residing in North Carolina, Dahlya offers transformative coaching, healing programs, retreats, and speaking engagements.

To learn more, Dahlya can be reached at dahlya@holisticmedicalhealing.com or holisticmedicalrehab@gmail.com. For courses and resources, including her free 3-part Brain Optimization Toolkit, visit www.holisticmedicalhealing.com.

# Going Beyond Pills & Protocols: Overcoming Dis-ease with Holistic Healthcare

## *Dahlya D. Shook*

*What if the key to extraordinary health, boundless energy, and unshakable resilience was already within you—waiting to be unlocked? Imagine breaking free from cycles of stress, pain, and exhaustion. Picture stepping into a life where you're not just surviving but thriving—stronger, wiser, and more vibrantly alive. What if the science of neuroplasticity, mind-body healing, and ancient energy medicine could merge with somatic transformation to create a path tailored for you—giving you the ability to reverse "dis-ease"?*

And what if the only thing standing between you and that reality was learning how to flip those switches?

I know what it's like to wake up every morning in pain, to feel like you're peeling yourself off the floor just to get through the day. The headaches, joint pain, brain fog, hair loss—they drain you. You push through, come home exhausted, crash, and repeat. And when your energy is gone, when your body is screaming at you but no one is listening, it takes a toll—on your self-trust, confidence, relationships, and life.

I also know the weight of being a burnt-out, depleted healthcare professional—pouring everything into helping others while silently falling apart. It's the kind of exhaustion that seeps into your bones, the quiet sacrifice no one sees. Caring for others while neglecting yourself is a slow unraveling.

But pain is not the end of this story. It was the catalyst that shattered the illusion that I was powerless over my health.

This was the breaking point that forced me to listen—to my body, intuition, and the medicine woman within me, the one who had walked this path in lifetimes before. She resurfaced in the depths of my suffering, guiding me to reclaim my wholeness, trust the wisdom in my cells, and rise stronger than before.

Through every flare-up, setback, and moment of doubt, I learned that healing wasn't about silencing the pain—it was about understanding it, working with it, and allowing it to reveal what needed to be transformed. My journey wasn't just about my restoration; it prepared me to help others reclaim theirs.

And now, I'm grateful because that pain led me here—to a place of power, purpose, and deep knowing that holistic wholeness is possible.

So, I tell you, there is another way—a way back to vitality, clarity, and strength. A client once told me that after our work together, she finally felt "the way she only dreamt of but could never make a reality on her own." I know your body is biologically wired to heal—you just need to learn how to support it.

I write this chapter to inspire those truly ready to reclaim their health and awaken the body's innate power to heal. You don't have to fight your body; you get to learn how to listen to it. Trust its whispers, support it with intention, and unlock the health you hope for.

For years, I believed I would always be sick in mind, body, or spirit. I trusted the traditional healthcare model, trapped in a cycle of emotional, physical, and mental struggle. I accepted sickness, fatigue, stress, and imbalance as unavoidable—something to be managed, not overcome. I believed I would always be at the mercy of anxiety, ADD, depression, disease, my circumstances, my genetics, and ancestral trauma. But what if the very model I trusted was the thing keeping me stuck?

Reactive medicine for chronic conditions doesn't just fail to heal—it perpetuates the trauma cycle, keeping us in survival mode rather than restoration. It conditions us to chase quick fixes, reinforcing stress, disconnection, and dependence instead of guiding us toward lasting transformation. This relentless cycle doesn't just keep us stuck—it makes the body sicker and ages it quicker. The constant stress response fuels inflammation and depletes energy, keeping us further from the vitality we seek.

Allow me to introduce myself. Like many of you, I once believed my health challenges were an unchangeable reality dictated by genetics and circumstance. I was certain that my DNA was my destiny and my doom.

Raised in Houston, Texas, in a household shaped by two profoundly different yet complementary influences. My father, an Australian brilliant neurologist, was deeply rooted in Western medicine and devoted to the science of the brain. My American mother, an intuitive and empathetic teacher, embodied emotional intelligence and deep sensitivity.

Neurology and neuroscience were introduced to me in ways most children never experience. I grew up hearing stories about a human brain encased in thick glass in the home—a symbol of my father's work. I would accompany him on hospital rounds, watching as he read MRIs and explained the complexities of brain function. As a young girl, this was where my fascination with neuroscience was born.

Science and intuition. Logic and feeling. The tangible and the unseen.

These opposing forces shaped me long before I understood their power. Medicine wasn't just a profession in our home—it was a way of life. An ache had a pill. A struggle had a prescription. This was the norm, the unquestioned path to wellness. Yet beneath this structured approach, something vital was missing.

At just 12 months old, my throat swelled shut, I turned blue, and I nearly died. That traumatic, autoimmune event left an imprint on my developing nervous system. My adaptive brain found a way to self-soothe—Trichotillomania, the compulsive urge to pull out one's hair. Years later, I would train in the very methods that helped me and others recover from it. If you or someone you know struggles with this behavior, there is holistic help available.

My near-death experience at 12 months old wasn't just trauma—it was a defining moment. In a split second where my body fought to survive, something deep within me awakened. That experience shaped me, instilling a resilience I would need for the challenges ahead. Because my path was never meant to be easy—it was meant to push me, to prepare me. And in that preparation, I found my purpose: to help others reclaim their strength, their health, and their lives.

By 15, I was diagnosed with learning disabilities and multiple mental health disorders, including debilitating anxiety and major depressive disorder. The solution? A cocktail of prescribed medications. Doctors assured me this was my only path forward. For over 20 years, I believed them. I followed the protocol, yet the symptoms persisted—cycling through emotions that made everyday life feel "hard." I remember one professional telling me, "Maybe this is as happy as you are supposed to be." This could not be the answer, but I did not know where else to go.

Though my nervous system bore the scars of that 12-month-old trauma, it also held the blueprint for healing. In its infinite adaptability, my brain found ways to cope—even if those ways seemed inexplicable to others. The compulsions, the behaviors, the subconscious survival mechanisms were all attempts at feeling safe, misunderstood by a medical system that had answers that weren't good enough. Decades later, I returned—not just to my body but to the work that was my purpose. I trained in the very methods that traditional healthcare had struggled to grasp. The very tools that helped me reclaim my life are now the ones I use to guide others back to their own.

So, in my overachieving trauma response way, I went back to school for higher education—determined to help others. I earned a Master's in Occupational Therapy, dedicating my career to restoring people's ability to live fully. I studied flow states, behavioral patterns, neurological conditions, and sensory integration. Yet the contradiction was impossible to ignore—I was guiding others toward engagement while I remained deeply disconnected from my own life.

Heavily medicated, numbed out, toxic with MRSA, bald, and battling depression, I was stuck in a cycle that felt impossible to break. I truly believed pharmaceuticals were the way forward.

A twist of fate introduced me to functional nutrition, and my health began to change. I began questioning everything I had been taught. I became my own experiment.

Early in my career, I worked with neurodevelopmental disorders, then moved into brain injury, mental health & stroke rehabilitation. I have been privileged to witness firsthand that healing is not just possible—it goes beyond what science can fully explain.

After over a decade in traditional healthcare, I saw both its necessity and limits. I loved my profession—it changed lives and gave me purpose. But I also saw patients trapped in an endless cycle—medications leading to side effects & more medications, while true healing was ignored. No one was talking about food as medicine or the body's innate power to renew. It was all damage control. I was trained to manage disease, but I choose to teach healing—because your body is designed and deserves far more than trauma response survival mode.

As I pursued advanced education in prevention, movement therapy, functional medicine, and holistic wellness, my eyes were opened—I could no longer unsee the truth. I didn't just learn—I applied. I personally integrated gut-healing protocols, nervous system techniques, and ancient practices. I discovered the profound relationship between the gut, the nervous system, and the entire body. The gut-brain axis is a powerful communicator, shaping mental, emotional, and physical well-being. Your body speaks in symptoms, sensations, and signals—true healing begins when you learn to listen.

The results were undeniable. I eliminated every pharmaceutical, reversed high cholesterol, cleared adult acne, healed carpal tunnel, regulated my sleep, and broke free from compulsive behaviors—hair pulling, nail biting, alcohol, and addiction. I finally quit smoking (again). My body and brain healed in ways traditional healthcare deemed impossible. Modern medicine prescribes pills—true healing comes from lifestyle medicine, functional nutrition, and nervous system resilience.

Naturally, this made for some interesting dinner conversations with my father. As I shared how I got off all my meds, he'd shake his head, half in fascination, half in disbelief. The neurophysiological debates that followed—especially about the gut-brain connection—were met with plenty of skepticism. But years later? He's now plant-based, living what I preach, and fully committed to longevity. Now that doctors are writing books about it, he's all ears—funny how a medical degree makes the truth more convincing!

Science is finally catching up with what ancient wisdom has always known. Epigenetics proves that our environment, thoughts, and stress levels shape gene expression. Polyvagal Theory reveals how trauma is stored in the nervous system and how breathwork restores balance. Your health isn't just about genetics; science confirms what ancient traditions have always known: the way you breathe, move, and fuel shape your health at every level.

Bringing this full circle, my journey with nervous system dysregulation began at just 12 months old when I nearly died. This early trauma imprinted itself in my body, shifting my nervous system into a state of constant stress. Modern and Eastern medicine agree that when the nervous system remains stuck in chronic stress, illness is inevitable.

True recovery isn't about masking symptoms—it's about understanding the body as a system, addressing root causes, and reclaiming resilience. At my "healthiest," I was checking all the boxes—yoga, juicing, clean eating, toxin-free living. But beneath it, I was running on unresolved trauma. When another crisis hit, old symptoms returned, and I spiraled again. It wasn't my habits that failed me—it was my nervous system. That was the missing piece. Health isn't just about what we do; it's about how we exist in our bodies. Once I learned to regulate my nervous system, I stopped fighting for health—I finally lived it.

Transformation happens when you stop managing symptoms and start understanding your body's wisdom. Your breath is medicine, your movement is therapy, and your touch is healing—your body holds the answers.

The nervous system is the foundation of our health, shaping how we experience stress, pain, and even joy. When we remain in prolonged states of fight-or-flight or shut down, our bodies respond with tension, inflammation, and imbalance—often manifesting in chronic pain, digestive issues, and emotional exhaustion. I've felt this firsthand, noticing tightness in my neck and belly as my body braced for the unknown. Your body remembers what your mind forgets. Healing begins when you listen. By integrating nervous system tools that shift us from survival mode into ventral vagal calm, we create the conditions for healing—where inflammation subsides, immunity strengthens, and clarity returns. When you lower the stress response, you create an environment to heal the symptoms.

My personal experiences, as well as patient/client journeys, led me to develop The RENEW Method, a multi-modal approach that supports deep, lasting transformation through:

- Resetting the nervous system with semantics and mindfulness.
- Energizing healing through movement and therapeutic modalities.
- Nourishing the body with targeted nutrition, gut health support, and detoxification.
- Elevating vitality with energy medicine and Reiki.
- Wisdom of holistic medicine, incorporating functional medicine and personalized supplementation.

This integrative practice not only transformed my health, happiness, and freedom but also helped others reclaim their vitality and step into the healthiest version of themselves. When this system is followed, something incredible happens. The symptoms a person thought they'd have forever—migraines, fatigue, hair loss, rashes, joint pain, mood swings, brain fog—disappear. And when those symptoms try to resurface, we no longer panic—because we know how to rebalance and trust that it is all happening for us to learn something new about ourselves or the world. We understand our own body.

Using my training & methods, I've had the privilege and honor to support a variety of people to go beyond traditional models:

- High-achieving entrepreneurs go from burnout to balance. Learning to regulate their bodies and minds, reducing their reliance on pharmaceuticals, and rediscovering joy in work and life.

- Executive CEOs, stressed over their children's anxiety, who find their family healthier and happier than they ever imagined.
- Veterans plagued by mental health struggles, hair-pulling, and autoimmune disorders who overcame challenges and became thriving entrepreneurs.
- Emotionally burnt-out healthcare professionals who found freedom, reclaiming health and lives.
- Entrepreneurs and Healers who did "everything right for their health" went from migraines and vertigo to clear heads.
- Children and adults with anxiety, sensory processing issues, learning to thrive academically and socially, engaging with families in ways that bring parents to tears.
- Car accident victims, written off by neurologists, who retrained their brains to engage in life and return to work—even as surgeons.
- Students labeled with ADD and panic disorders, struggling in therapy, who healed skin-picking and hair-pulling and went on to attend colleges their parents once thought impossible.
- Young women diagnosed with PCOS who thought they would never conceive—experiencing healthy pregnancies.
- Adults with seizure disorders who learned to feel safe in their bodies post-diagnosis.

And the list goes on.

I share these examples to show you that anyone can transform.

In a world where sickness has become the norm and speaking out against traditional models is frowned upon, I stand with a movement of practitioners, functional medicine specialists, energy healers, and Reiki Masters who are shifting the paradigm—educating, empowering, and teaching you how to become your own self-healer.

Through my international group programs, private virtual coaching, and transformational retreats, I guide people through my five-step system to master their health and experience vitality and freedom from "dis-ease" in ways they only imagined.

However, the most profound transformations don't happen in isolation but in community. Teaching on large stages, at conferences, and retreats accelerates healing. When people come together with a shared intention to heal, something powerful ignites. They realize they are not alone. They shift from hopeless to empowered, from stuck to limitless. They step into a new identity—one rooted in wellness, freedom, and the ability to live fully.

Transformation isn't just about gaining more information—it's about embodiment. I guide people beyond knowledge into their bodies, into the safe spaces of their nervous systems. In those moments, they access a deep inner reserve, a knowing that once felt unreachable. I've heard people say, "It feels like I'm coming home." And I know this to be true for myself as well.

Because when you surround yourself with a community that prioritizes health, you don't just change—you create a ripple effect. More energy. More freedom. More choices. More LIFE. This is what it means to truly thrive.

This is the power of healing and the power of YOU. Through this work, you reclaim your vitality and live the life you were always meant to lead. This is the real healthcare. The greatest medicine isn't found outside of you—it's in your ability to regulate, restore, and realign with your own nature.

I am profoundly grateful that this transformational book found its way into your hands. The insights within have the power to shift not just how you think, feel, and act but also how you lead, create, and embody your highest potential. True well-being isn't just about feeling good; it's about radiating unshakable confidence, deep resilience, and a vitality that fuels every aspect of your life.

My mission is to ensure that these foundational resources are accessible to all because everyone deserves to operate at their fullest capacity—mentally, physically, and emotionally.

On my website, www.holisticmedicalhealing.com, you'll find a wealth of emotional and physical health resources, including a free Three-Step Brain Optimization Toolkit designed to enhance clarity, energy, and overall performance.

If you're ready to step into a higher level of personal mastery—or if you know someone who would benefit from this work—I invite you to reach out. You can connect with me at Dahlya@holisticmedicalhealing.com or visit www.holisticmedicalhealing.com.

Your physiology follows your focus. Where attention goes, energy flows—so choose wisely

\*\*\*

Dahlya Brown Shook, OTR, MOT, CMHIMP, CHC

dahlya@holisticmedicalhealing.com

holisticmedicalrehab@gmail.com

www.holisticmedicalhealing.com

# Ariyana Eira

Certified Transformational Life Coach, Spiritual Life Coach and Meditation Instructor (Mindvalley-Evercoach, 2022).

CPD Level 7 Diploma in Counselling Skills Mentor-Practitioner

Published under author names Ariyana Eira and Eira Stuart.

Eclosion Coaching UK- Aurora Life Design.

Scholarship Trainee in Trauma Studies with Dr Bessel Van Der Kolk at the Trauma Research Foundation

Creative Writer at Nightingale and Sparrow, Indie Blu(e) Publishing, Vociferous Press.

Patient Advocacy Writer (2019-Present)

M.E. Association, registered UK Charity.

https://m.facebook.com/EclosionCoaching-by-Ariyana-Eira-109987791648035

# Suffering as a Conduit to Self-Knowledge and Unconditional Love

## By Ariyana Eira

*This chapter is dedicated to the world, to my human family. We may feel at times we are separate, but we are all part of one universal consciousness and life force.*

*You are a spark of divine consciousness made manifest into physical form; remember who you are.*

In Western society, we are often taught that our worth comes from our achievements and what we **do**. We forget that we are infused with a spark of divine consciousness, that we were made in God's image, and that life has a creational purpose and spiritual meaning. It is who we **are** that matters.

I have observed a lack of meaning, trajectory and emptiness in modern society, a kind of existential crisis, where many seem to be disconnected from an awareness or relationship with a divine energy, creational power and consequently, from the life force within them; from a state, or spiritual void, namely in the Nietzschean sense, or even in terms of the Cartesian dialectic of rationalism and body mind separation.

Could hell, in fact, be a state of separation from the source of all creation? From the well-spring spark of divinity within us? From a feeling or belief in destiny and a sense of purpose, of intentional divine orchestration, and from our very existence and that of the world?

Life is a miracle. If all people thought this way and truly appreciated, valued, and honoured this gift, perhaps less people would suffer and feel so disconnected from themselves, from God, the divine presence, society, one another and from having meaning and purpose in life.

I've been through some of the most extreme rings of fire, dark night of the soul experiences that few people encounter in a lifetime, let alone so young. This has given me a unique perspective on life, gained from the abyss of unimaginable suffering.

When I was in my early twenties, I had a horse-riding accident. I flew backward off a half-wild horse while attempting a jump, immediately losing consciousness on impact. For the next four years, my limitless spirit was consigned to a body with limitations. I have always had a passion and vision for life and a recognition of myself as boundless and eternal. The word "can't" **never** existed in my vocabulary until now.

I tried physiotherapy, neuro-physiotherapy, osteopathy, needle therapy/ myofascial release, traditional remedies, and acupuncture (despite my aversion to needles), to name but a few. Finally, my physiotherapist suggested I may have "chronic fatigue syndrome."

- *"Great! Now she's making up a "syndrome" to justify my lack of progression,"* I thought.

After multiple referrals, finally, a hospital stay, a diagnosis, and a standstill. I conceded, understanding that there was no further to push to **do**; it was time to **BE**. Sometimes, success is knowing when to stop and having the discernment to do so, which is also a success, not a failure.

Receiving my diagnosis dealt a second blow. I was no longer recovering from/ rehabilitating and managing the after-effects of an injury, but a young woman with a long-term "incurable" illness, misunderstood and stigmatised, often disbelieved, by medics themselves; one of whom pointedly informed me that "M.E. doesn't exist," that is, until a top London consultant affirmed that it most certainly **did** exist and had an undeniable biomedical organic origin.

I went through an exceedingly difficult period. I became completely incapacitated in a nursing home, blind and paralysed (for eight years) with a rare biomedical neurological-immune condition that has been highly politicised and stigmatised for decades due to a lack of research funding.

There was also a deliberate attempt by the insurance industry in the United States of America in the 1970s to reclassify the neurological disease Myalgic Encephalomyelitis (M.E.), listed since the 1930s by the World Health Organisation under the classification of Neurological diseases (G93.3), reducing it to a trivialising, clinical syndrome ( a recognisable pattern of symptoms, namely fatigue).

This is how terms like "yuppie flu" were coined back in the 1980s and where the stigma began. In reality, M.E. stands for Myalgic Encephalomyelitis, a neurological-immunological disease that causes low-grade encephalitis in the brain and spine, including muscle pain, muscle metabolism, and dysfunction.

I was asleep twenty-three hours a day and could only maintain consciousness for twenty minutes three times a day for essential care to keep me alive. I was in a constant state of sensory overload, an excruciating symptom and feeling of static scrambling in my brain, like the old analogue televisions on a channel with no signal, making a constant *"shhhhhh"* whooshing sound, ears ringing, and sensory hyperarousal.

My brain felt like it was being bombarded; every noise was a log on the fire, and everything had a reddish hue, as though my eyes were bleeding internally. I had a constant migraine, my skin burning to the touch. Lights burned, causing stabbing pain in my spine (even if I covered my eyes), exposure to light seemed to have inflamed my rib cage/ intercostal muscles (Costochondritis), making me feel like I was wearing a tight corset while inhaling sand, which suffocated my lungs every time I inhaled (no, this wasn't anxiety).

What began with a feeling of seasickness from a viral inner ear infection (Labyrinthitis) developed into severe vertigo, then dysautonomia. Even while lying in bed, I felt as though I was on a rocking boat; if I turned my head to the right, the whole room would start spinning. This progressed into feelings of falling backward and through the bed symptoms, including descriptions best kept to oneself or else risk sinister inferences from doctors who didn't even believe in the biomedical basis for the illness. let alone entertain abstract descriptions about "rocking like a boat," feeling "like I'm on fire" waking up feeling "like I'm underwater unable to breathe." Doctors who don't believe in M.E. tend to view it as "medically unexplained" or "functional" (physical manifestation of psychological symptoms); neither of these are correct.

I had severe noise sensitivity. I could not bear the sound of a voice. I was severely sensitive to light; I would convulse or tremble, suffering from seizures and migraines. Exposure to light would make my skin and spine burn in the same way as when you're sunburnt and can't even endure the feeling of fabric against your skin. Even in the dark with covered eyes, I still saw bright light as though I was looking into the sun.

The lesson that can be learned from the situation of one who is limited by chronic illness, disability, or infirmity may be to serve to show the value of human-***being***: that we each have value by virtue of who we **are**, not what we **do** and that, in itself, creates the frequency and potentiality for those values and for you, as an individuated spark of divine consciousness, made manifest-embodied soul, to exist.

Self-actualization is an aspect of the attitudes and responsibilities of spiritual and self-mastery. Self-sovereignty is another. Self-actualization can be achieved through prayer, meditation, and cultivating mindfulness. This involves being aware of the present moment and learning to live fully within it; being aware of every thought, and every action, and maintaining a posture of engaged detachment; being aware of our surroundings without getting "sucked in" to any drama, power dynamics or trigger attempts from others, or allowing them to affect us. We must remain in control of how we feel and react and refrain from giving power to anything that disempowers us or causes us to lose our inner/ vertical connection.

We are always accountable for how we direct our energy and how we respond. However, we are created with a residual, or superimposed, reptilian complex/ goat brain, which can have an impact and cause involuntary knee jerk, fight, or flight reactions. These originate from the limbic primal brain complex. We can, of course, control and integrate it, but this, too, is directly related to how conscious and spiritually aware we are and how far we can exercise and embody personal responsibility and mastery.

I was definitely challenged in this regard. Firstly, because I had an energy-limiting illness made worse by exertion, which meant I had severe limits on my ability to be conscious, let alone functional. My second challenge came when I found myself in a situation of vulnerability and dependence on others yet began to endure less favourable and adverse treatment from them.

Self-mastery in such a situation is not always easy, particularly with symptoms that can easily skyrocket, especially if certain protocols and attitudes are not maintained. However, with patience, perseverance, and forgiveness for when we fail, we can begin to embark on the journey of unlearning habitual responses and cultivating a stance of taking a step back in self-observant engaged detachment. Part of this process also involves recognising the free will choice of others to misuse their free will, divorced from their divine potential.

We cannot control the actions of others, but we can choose our response, and we can choose the power we give others to "upset," "hurt," or incite an emotional response in us when this may only fuel the adverse behaviour by giving it power. Withdraw your consent to give power to attempts to trigger, disempower, or engage you in lower vibrational dynamics.

Even if you are incapacitated, your stated intention and what you embody makes a difference. Like attracts like and if you align your stance and frequency integrity with your desired probability reality outcome and best self-potential, the more of that you attract and become. Remove any identification with victimhood. This is a powerful first step, even if you are in such a state, start with yourself, state your intention, become that vibration.

This is how, in our BE-ing-ness, our presence (as instruments of divine grace, as anchor points for divine will) and frequency integrity/ embodiment create ripples throughout the world, touching those around us and the quantum field itself; even in illness and incapacity, if we choose this path of impeccability.

The path of personal mastery is about being impeccable with your word, embodying your values, and taking responsibility for your manifest reality in the aspects you can control. You may not be able to change the circumstances, but you always have choices and control over how you respond. Therein lies your power. Therein lay my power, even in incapacity, due to the fact that I still had the power to choose my responses and how I used my limited energy.

These virtues, attitudes and responsibilities of mastery may be readily assimilated in theory, but in practice, when you're bed bound and paralysed in a nursing home, completely reliant on caregivers, with loved ones far away, unable to talk, defend yourself, or use a phone. It becomes a whole different story, especially when experiencing adversity and mistreatment from the very people entrusted with your "care," health, and well-being.

So, how do you stand in your power and sovereignty when incapacitated and dependent on others, particularly in adversity?

It seems like a rather cruel test. However, true mastery is about personal responsibility embodiment and realising the attitudes and responsibilities of mastery on ALL levels and in ALL situations (become the eye of the storm).

Firstly, when you remove your need for validation and approval from external sources, you break free from deriving your own self-worth from them, including people's judgements and (mis) perceptions. You, therefore, simultaneously reclaim your power and sovereignty back from them and cease to give others that power. When you learn not to give your power away, you also end the cycle of feeding into certain dynamics. For example, if someone is trying to trigger you, remove your energy by not engaging. Remain calm and centered in the eye of the storm (of non-engagement and engaged detachment), anchored in self-knowledge.

You are whom you vibrationally embody yourself to be, whom you vibrationally harmonise yourself to be. No one else defines you but you in your vibrational offering and vibrational co-resonance.

When we heal unhealthy patterns and responses, we create a new divinely aligned emotional, behavioural model and reality, not only for ourselves, but for others and for those of us raising a new generation, through our lived example. Our personal attitudes and embodiment of integrity are therefore far reaching, creating a ripple effect in all who interact with us.

Engaging with misdirected energy at you would be to engage and empower a victim/victimizer blame game dynamic, where blame is thrown back and forth in the transference of power and between a "victim" target and an aggressor/perpetrator "victimizer." There's a difference between taking a stand and not engaging in attempts to trigger you and take you out of your power and between engaging your energy quantum, attention, and power in a low vibrational victim-victimizer dynamic/game.

Creating a boundary is not a V-V game; neither is taking a stand. Both are stances in personal power without encroaching on the free will choice of another person. Wisdom and discernment are knowing the difference.

I have often asked God and listened to the voice of intuition inside me during those challenging times and asked myself. Why? How do you stand in your power when you are seemingly powerless? Is this what Jesus meant when he said: "My strength is made perfect in weakness" (Holy Bible, Corintheans 12:9). The inner knowing within me replied: *to learn a lesson in sovereignty.*

Building a relationship with the Divine intelligence is entwined with the process of self-knowledge because I AM a part of the creator and was created by its Divine spark. I AM a drop in the ocean that is the eternal divine well spring, first field intelligence -consciousness; and the voice of intuition inside me originates from this source of consciousness. Therefore, the process of self-knowledge and uncovering our mission and purpose is intrinsic to aligning with divine will.

The idea is to connect to our soul, to our divinity, to the light of God within us, reclaim and stand in our sovereignty, and carry this light as a beacon, as a truth in all that we do, to be the instruments of divine will and to be a conduit of the divine energy made manifest in physical form. When you do this, you enter into a flow state/elevated state of consciousness where events begin to align, and you begin to enter into a state of harmony and frequency co-resonance and alignment with divine will and universal service.

One way I was able to stand in my power, in a practical sense, was through setting boundaries. At the nursing home, I had a team of support assistants, and I was able to have a say, to a certain extent, to who was allowed into my space and into contact with me.

Secondly, I had a formal mental capacity assessment which protected me legally, as a person with the mental capacity to make their own decisions, despite being severely incapacitated, blind, and paralysed for over seven years. No care professional could impose any protocol or even touch me without my consent. I, therefore, also had the right to choice and control in my care and beyond. This didn't stop certain malicious individuals from twisting policy and using it against me through institutional bureaucracy, playing mind and power games, including misusing their authority as team leaders.

One of these "professionals" was a lead nurse who qualified in the 1970s when M.E. was highly stigmatised, and therefore didn't "believe in it." She consequently ventured to give me a hard time every chance she got, from telling my carers my illness was psychological and was my "choice to lay in bed" because I "don't try" and "don't want to help myself" that my needs were not a priority, declaring feeding me was a "low skill job." She proceeded to send me the most inexperienced, unfamiliar carers who didn't have the skill, training, or ability to care for me safely. This put me at risk of choking. They couldn't even understand or communicate with me as I was non-verbal. However, there was still a level of autonomy and rights that protected me, which would have been far more detrimental if I didn't have mental capacity.

In 2005 a young thirty-two-year-old woman named Sophia Mirza became the first UK recorded case of death from M.E. Her doctors didn't believe in M.E. and, in the end, sectioned/committed her under the Mental Health Act. She was eventually released after the involvement of a human rights lawyer. However, she died at home very soon after her release, due to acute renal failure arising from M.E. and the adverse conditions and treatment she was subjected to on the secure psychiatric ward (exposure to light, denied physical care, etc.).

Twenty years later and despite a much campaigned for victory, in the form of a change in clinical policy, both in the USA in 2015 with the recognition of M.E. by the Department of Human Services and the National Academy of Medicine as a systemic disease and in 2021 in the UK, these types of scenarios continue, even in hospitals where M.E. Patients are denied NG feeding tubes and are left to die of malnutrition. An inquest was held recently regarding a young woman who died in this manner (name withheld for confidentiality).

There are at least two other known cases at present in U.K. hospitals battling against a similar fate.

So, is there any virtue in suffering? In short, no. Suffering is not a virtue. Even though the notion of self-sacrifice has formed part of ingrained cultural programming in western society, suffering, and illness may have a message to the world:

Suffering can be a conduit to profound healing, personal growth, and spiritual transformation. However, so can love. The act of caregiving requires stepping out of the self and meeting the other person where they are at. This requires love, compassion, and empathy, which can radiate and elevate the suffering into a space of healing.

Other times, it is pointless, and those suffering are merely a reflection of a broken world, a by-product of the absence of love, compassion, effective action, selfishness, and neglect of others. In this case, suffering is part of the cause and effect of the misuse of free will that then has an effect on us collectively, whether directly or consequentially; revealing within the microcosm the disconnect and the brokenness in the macrocosm of the consensus reality/world.

Suffering, in some cases, can be part of a healing process that purifies and alchemises by bringing attention to certain situations or areas of healing within us. Think of a detox, wherein you are sick and purging to ultimately be healthy. This involves a period of suffering, which can be a form of processing through "karmic" cycles or life lessons to bring about that personal growth or healing.

Even in the case of abuse (which is never acceptable), consider the perspective that abusers get triggered because they observe something in the person, they target that is lacking in them or that they envy in others. Witnessing suffering may serve as a trigger wherein lies a hidden lesson. It creates an opportunity for cultivating compassion and self-awareness toward personal growth. Alternatively, it brings remembrance of their own frailty and the fact that this can easily be their situation if they get ill or have an accident. The individual's response to either lash out and resist the mirror that the suffering is reflecting or embrace the triggering situation to develop self-awareness, and personal growth is an individual choice. In order for the world to be a harmonious place, we must all choose to collectively embody certain values, virtues, attitudes, and responsibilities so that they manifest in the collective consciousness consensus reality.

Many think that an individual cannot make a difference. That is not the case. We are each a drop that creates the mighty ocean/ collective consciousness. Each of us is a beacon that contributes toward the manifest reality we collectively experience.

Suffering offers us the opportunity, as a society, to develop and exercise compassion, to see a reflection of our own impermanence and to be humbled, grateful for the gift of life and to be mindful to live a conscious, worthwhile life, using our gifts to contribute to the world and to uplift it and serve others.

In the western Christian tradition, the central focus mission and purpose in life is love. This is a common factor in all faiths and spiritual traditions, which may serve as a common ground for establishing a dynamic of interconnection toward unity consciousness. I would add to this by saying not only love, but pure, unconditional love, and a step further, omni love in unity consciousness that recognizes us all as part of one interconnected human family, as individuated sparks emanating from one divine wellspring. Unity consciousness is the natural state of being. We are ONE, a mirror of the All-Oneness.

Love is the answer, the ultimate healer, and the ultimate reason and purpose of our existence. Let everything you do flow from love. Let your presence uplift others, and as my master coach teacher, Mr Ajit Nawalka of Evercoach, used to say: "Always serve with love."

My main mission as a Transformational and Spiritual Life coach, is to commit to my own personal development to be in my highest expression, to realise my full potential and to support you, all who co-create with me, to do the same. My vision in service is to support you in your re-awakening of your true authentic self and to hold space for you in your journey of discovering your personal vision-mission, to fulfill your own unique path, purpose, and destiny in this lifetime (regardless of whether you are on a spiritual path or not).

Remember who you are as a soul essence infused with a spark of divine consciousness/ light made manifest. Live consciously in harmony with your fellow man, being mindful that every action has a ripple effect, both directly and indirectly, in the consensus reality. Live to be a vessel and conduit of unconditional love, divine love and remember, that the purpose of life is to give life a purpose.

I am grateful for the opportunity that has brought us together to connect on this page. I would be honoured and happy to co-create with you and support you on your journey.

With love and blessings,

Ariyana Eira

With gratitude to Mr. Britt and J. Lutes for this opportunity, collaboration, and your support; to Mr. Tiyagi for your support and encouragement; and to my fellow *"The Change"* co-authors on this project. It's been an honour and a pleasure co-creating with you all.

\*\*\*

Contact:

AriyanaEira@hotmail.com

LinkedIn: https://www.linkedin.com/in/ariyana-eira-stuart-777331234

Donation links to support M.E. Research:

U.K:

Invest in M.E. Research:

https://www.investinme.org/fund.shtml

U.S.A.:

https://med.stanford.edu/sgtc.html

https://www.omf.ngo/?form=donatenow

Coach Member of The Self-Love Network:

https://theselflove.network/members/10370593

Medium:

https://medium.com/@ariyanaeira/

Link Tree:

https://linktr.ee/ariyanaeira

Publications:

Individual:

Stuart, E. (2020) *Eudaimonia*. (KDP).

https://www.amazon.co.uk/Eudaimonia-Eira-Stuart/dp/B08R495424/ref=mp_s_a_1_1?crid=2QRNF7HJ8MF1E&dib=eyJ2IjoiMSJ9.VIh2LsCsoITvPbzQfcN61A.QtU7-OEsSwGkX7P5HkKCKSMsif9UkjCTsn-al2Wev34&dib_tag=se&keywords=eira+stuart+eudaimonia&qid=1742189003&sprefix=eira+stuart+eudaimonia%2Caps%2C59&sr=8-1

Stuart, E. (2020) *Metanoia*, (KDP).

https://www.amazon.co.uk/Metanoia-Eira-Stuart/dp/B08JV9JZ1W/ref=mp_s_a_1_1?crid=1T0BM6T7765ST&dib=eyJ2IjoiMSJ9.g4hQ51SQ8_TZz6tKLdlWYg.bI3_vgzTiKB1d6g3CoYDtWEZzqlvjACTIA41shEEFh8&dib_tag=se&keywords=eira+stuart+metanoia&qid=1742188898&sprefix=eira+stuart+metanoia%2Caps%2C96&sr=8-1

Collaborative:

Stuart, E., *M.E.* in Christine E. Ray (ed.), But *You Don't Look Sick*, Indie Blu(e) Publishing, November 2021.

https://indieblu.net/category/but-you-dont-look-sick/

Stuart, E., *Severe M.E.; A Conundrum in Care* (2020), in Crowhurst, G.(ed), *More Notes for Carers*. Chapter 14, P.85 More Notes for Carers and M.E. Essentials Journal. October 2020.

https://www.amazon.co.uk/More-Notes-Carers-Greg-Crowhurst/dp/1716384532/ref=mp_s_a_1_1?crid=21LWC8JPUXUPL&dib=eyJ2IjoiMSJ9.YLPPlj5fzDgxacV9PeAFzg.2rgYzJR4AAFBHkKbCWkgRsHA581DVDs0iKFUjemNbxE&dib_tag=se&keywords=more+notes+for+carers&qid=1742189649&sprefix=more+notes+for+carers%2Caps%2C76&sr=8-1

Stuart, E. *Perception and Perspective in* (2020) in Seabock, J.(ed.), *Screaming from the Silence; An Anonymous Anthology.* Vociferous Press, January 2020).

https://nightingaleandsparrow.com/screaming-from-the-silence/

*The Change*[23]

https://www.goodreads.com/book/show/51297089-screamong-from-the-silence

# Dr. R Harrison Baxter

R. Harrison Baxter is a globally recognized transformational leadership expert, keynote speaker, and author of *The Reflective Advantage*. A master facilitator and corporate trainer, Baxter brings more than a decade of experience in helping individuals and organizations unlock high-impact leadership through reflective listening, neuroscience, and emotional intelligence.

Grounded in traditional values and a forward-thinking approach, his work bridges boardroom performance and human connection. He is also the founder of the Bronx Rebels Northeast Elite—a football leadership initiative that partners with the Kenyan Football Federation of American Football and the international organization iChange Nations, bringing American Football the Africa. Through this work, Baxter cultivates discipline, empowerment, and global citizenship among youth leaders.

Named one of the Global Game Changers of 2024, Baxter's legacy is rooted in resilience—growing up in the Bronx during the crack epidemic and rising to become a global voice in leadership transformation. His Listen to Lead Suite equips leaders to shift from reaction to reflection, from control to connection, and from noise to true influence.

Whether he's training executives, mentoring emerging leaders, or coaching on the gridiron, Baxter's mission remains the same: to create a world where leadership begins with listening—and transforms lives from the inside out.

# The Mirror Within: A Journey to Empowerment through Reflective Leadership Prologue: Why This Story Matters

### By Dr. R Harrison Baxter

Leadership isn't just about vision decks, revenue growth, or corner offices. It's about human beings who sit quietly in meetings, wondering if they matter. It's about the voices that speak up—only to be dismissed. It's about the pressure to perform, produce, and power through, even when your spirit is running on empty.

This is not just Maya Carter's story—it's the story of millions of professionals who have confused volume for value, performance for presence, and productivity for purpose.

We live in a world wired for noise—but it's reflective leadership that creates the resonance. Neuroscience confirms what wisdom traditions have always taught: the brain rewires in response to safety, empathy, and deep listening. Yet we teach leaders to talk more, push harder, and never pause.

This story is a call back to the pause.

It's a reminder that the most transformational leadership doesn't roar—it reflects. It doesn't command—it listens. It doesn't control—it empowers.

And in a world hungry for authentic connection, reflective listening is no longer a soft skill. It's a survival skill. It's a strategy. It's a revolution.

## The Breaking Point

Maya Carter had built her life like a skyscraper—impressive on the outside, but hollow inside. Her calendar overflowed with titles, accolades, and deadlines—but her soul remained threadbare. She was a mid-level executive at a Fortune 500 company, known for her sharp mind, tireless drive, and ruthless efficiency. But somewhere between the boardrooms and the burnout, Maya had lost her voice.

She spoke in meetings but rarely felt heard. She issued instructions yet rarely felt understood. The louder she pushed, the more invisible she became. At home, her relationships were fraying. Her partner had once said, half-jokingly, "You're here, but you're never really *with* me." The words haunted her.

Her days had become mechanical—early alarms, back-to-back Zooms, strategy meetings that felt more like staged performances. Even in team check-ins, Maya found herself talking *at* people, not *with* them. There was no connection, just execution.

She remembered when she first started her career—fresh out of business school, idealistic and passionate. Back then, she believed leadership was about inspiration. Now, it felt more like survival.

Then came the quarterly review. She had poured herself into the company's latest initiative—late nights, early mornings, zero margin for error. But when her VP skimmed over her contribution with a cursory "Good work," before moving on to another topic, something in her clenched. Not in a dramatic outburst—just a quiet, internal collapse. Her voice clenched in her throat, and for the first time in years, she had nothing to say. Not because she was speechless, but because she was tired of screaming into silence.

Later that evening, she sat alone in her car, keys in hand, engine off, staring at her reflection in the rearview mirror. She didn't recognize the woman staring back. "I don't want to live like this," she whispered. Not another year. Not another month. Not another day.

**The Unexpected Mentor**

Change often arrives disguised as inconvenience. For Maya, it came in the form of a mandatory leadership retreat—an offsite in the mountains hosted by a facilitator she had never heard of: Jordan Wells. The internal email promised "transformational leadership through reflective practices." Maya rolled her eyes. She expected corporate platitudes, role-play exercises, and team-building games involving ropes and trust falls.

What she didn't expect was a masterclass in human connection.

Jordan was unlike any facilitator she'd ever met. No booming voice, no flashy slides. He stood with calm authority, letting silence work harder than sound. He introduced the retreat with one statement:

"We're not here to fix your leadership. We're here to help you *find* it."

The neuroscience came on day one, woven in with stories and metaphors. Jordan explained the mirror neuron system—the brain's built-in capacity for empathy. "When you truly listen reflectively," he said, "you're literally activating the other person's brain to feel safe, seen, and heard. That safety rewires behavior. That's the science behind trust."

Maya took notes, half intrigued, half skeptical. But it was the practice that hooked her.

During a paired listening exercise, Maya was instructed to simply reflect what her partner said—not analyze, not fix, not redirect. Just mirror. She found herself uncomfortable in the silence. But when her partner, a quiet marketing manager, teared up after sharing a challenge and said, "That's the first time I've felt heard all week," Maya froze. Something clicked.

Later that evening, Jordan shared a phrase that would stay with her forever: "Reflective leadership is not a tactic. It's a way of seeing people—and letting them see themselves."

Maya didn't know it yet, but this retreat was not just about leading teams differently. It was about relearning how to lead *herself*.

## The Learning Curve

Maya returned to work different—not drastically, but undeniably. She started small. She initiated one-on-one check-ins that weren't tied to deliverables, but to well-being. She asked questions like, "What's something that's been heavy on your mind this week?" and "What's not being said in this room that needs to be heard?"

She began experimenting with micro-reflections during meetings: simple restatements like, "What I'm hearing is that this deadline feels unrealistic given the resources." Colleagues were taken aback—but positively. People leaned in more. Dialogue replaced directives.

At one staff meeting, an idea proposed by a junior team member was quickly dismissed by a senior colleague. Maya stepped in—not to defend or mediate, but to reflect. "Let's pause—what I heard was a suggestion rooted in innovation. Maybe we need to hear that again through a different lens." That simple redirection changed the tone of the conversation.

People started seeking her out, not for decisions, but for clarity. One teammate said, "You have a way of creating space that makes people want to speak truthfully."

Maya also started seeing subtle shifts in herself. She didn't rush to fill silences. She was no longer addicted to performance. She noticed when she was posturing—and paused instead of pushing through.

What surprised her most was how much more effective her team became. Less confusion. Less rework. Less burnout. Reflective listening, it turned out, was not a soft skill—it was a performance accelerator.

She began collecting feedback—not on what she was doing, but on how people were experiencing her. The shift was profound. Words like "trustworthy," "grounding," and "empathetic" replaced "sharp," "assertive," and "driven."

Her leadership style hadn't weakened—it had deepened. And her influence, once measured by volume, was now measured by resonance.

**The Inner Mirror**

The most radical shift in Maya's leadership didn't happen in the boardroom. It happened in the quiet moments—late evenings with her journal, early morning walks without earbuds, and the unspoken conversations she had with herself. Reflective listening had begun as a practice she used with others. Now, it had become her tool for self-reconnection.

She no longer dismissed discomfort or numbed anxiety with productivity. She leaned in and listened—without judgment. When her inner critic whispered, *you're not doing enough,* she paused and responded internally: *It sounds like I'm afraid I'll lose worth if I slow down.*

This self-dialogue became a powerful shift in her emotional intelligence. Jordan's neuroscience teachings echoed in her reflections. The prefrontal cortex—her brain's executive function—

was gaining strength through mindfulness and meta-cognition. The amygdala, once triggered easily by pressure and perfectionism, had less control over her decisions.

Her leadership was no longer reactive—it was responsive.

Maya began tracking patterns—not just in meetings, but in her inner world. What triggers her urgency? What sparks her self-doubt? What environments nourish her confidence?

She started building rituals—not just routines. A 10-minute "listening pause" at the start of each workday, where she reflected on three things: her emotional tone, her internal narratives, and her intention for the day.

She also started writing letters she never sent—to past versions of herself. One began, "To the Maya who thought hustle was the price of belonging: You were doing your best. But you deserve more than survival."

This wasn't fluff. This was neuroscience-backed empowerment. Studies showed that self-reflective writing and intentional emotional labeling increase neuroplasticity and strengthen self-leadership. Maya had unknowingly turned her life into a laboratory of transformation.

When a conflict arose with a senior leader in a budget meeting, Maya noticed her instinct to defend herself sharply. But she paused, took a breath, and asked, "What's the real tension underneath this conversation for both of us?" The room went silent. Then, the breakthrough happened—not in the numbers, but in honesty.

She was no longer just managing projects. She was modeling presence. And people followed—not because she demanded respect, but because she reflected trust.

**The Empowered Life**

Empowerment didn't mean Maya became someone new. It meant she finally became fully herself. She wasn't chasing validation or climbing for applause. She was rising with purpose—and reaching back to lift others as she did.

She launched a monthly leadership circle within her organization—not just another workshop series, but a space for real conversations. It began with six people. No agendas. No PowerPoints. Just presence. The rules were simple: speak your truth, listen with intention, and reflect without judgment. It wasn't just a program—it became a movement.

People showed up. Not for snacks or checkboxes, but for the atmosphere. One senior manager said, "This is the first space I've been in where I didn't feel like I had to wear armor." Another said, "This circle doesn't just sharpen my skills—it restores my spirit."

Maya started bringing in excerpts from her journal, sometimes reading them aloud to the group. She wasn't trying to teach from a pedestal—she was leading through vulnerability. That transparency cracked open deeper trust within her team than years of performance reviews ever had.

Outside work, she began mentoring young professionals, particularly women navigating leadership roles with quiet insecurity. One mentee, Rachel, a bright analyst fresh out of grad school, came to her in tears one day. "I feel like I have to act like someone else just to be taken seriously," she confessed.

Maya didn't offer a textbook solution. She leaned forward and said, "What would it look like if you trusted your voice more than your fear?"

Then she paused and mirrored Rachel's words: "It sounds like you're not afraid of failing—you're afraid of not being seen for who you really are."

Rachel broke down. Not because it was new—but because, finally, it was reflected back.

That moment wasn't just a coaching success. It was a passing of the torch. Maya realized that leadership wasn't a title. It was a legacy of presence.

But Maya also saw a contrasting arc. Kevin, a colleague with a similar tenure and skillset, took the opposite path. Resistant to change, he doubled down on command-and-control leadership. He saw vulnerability as weakness and listening as inefficiency. His team began to burn out. Turnover rose. Kevin blamed the talent pool.

Maya saw the writing on the wall. The difference wasn't intelligence or experience—it was presence. Leadership that reflects empowers. Leadership that dictates exhausts.

Maya thought often about what Jordan had said: "Reflective leadership is a way of seeing people—and letting them see themselves." Now, she was that mirror for others, just as he had been for her.

And Maya's own reflection had changed too. One day, during a quiet moment, she looked in the mirror again—not the rearview kind, but the one in her hallway at home. And this time, she smiled.

She saw a woman who had unlearned the myth of perfection, rewired her relationship with self-worth, and reclaimed her voice—not by speaking louder, but by listening deeper.

She pulled out her journal and wrote a final note to herself:

"To the Maya who once doubted her worth—thank you for holding on. You didn't break. You evolved. And now, you lead with grace, not grit."

Her life wasn't perfect. Challenges still came. But she faced them with a steadiness she never knew she had. Because now, her power came from presence—not position. Her leadership came from listening—not lecturing.

She decided to write an article titled The Neuroscience of Reflective Listening: Why It Changes More Than Conversations. She referenced studies on neuroplasticity, emotional labeling, and how reflective pauses enhance cognitive regulation. The article gained traction across leadership platforms and was eventually featured in a global leadership summit.

In her closing keynote, Maya ended not with a quote from a scholar or guru—but from her own journal:

"Empowerment is not a volume knob. It's a tuning fork. The more deeply you hear yourself, the more clearly others will hear you."

She left the audience with three reflection questions:

- Who do you become when no one is watching?
- What parts of your voice have you silenced to fit in?
- Where in your life can you replace reaction with reflection?

And every time she paused, reflected, and responded with clarity, she lived her new mantra:

"The better you listen, the stronger you lead. And the stronger you lead... the better you live."

## Epilogue: The Ripple Effect

Months after Maya's keynote, the impact continued to ripple outward. Her article on reflective listening sparked a series of roundtables in organizations across industries. Leaders began integrating reflective pauses into performance reviews, onboarding programs, and even project debriefs. One Fortune 100 executive wrote to her, "You helped me realize I'd been leading from a pedestal instead of a presence."

Maya didn't seek the spotlight. But when you carry a mirror, people see themselves more clearly—and they remember who handed it to them.

She continued mentoring, writing, and facilitating. Her leadership circle became a model replicated in over 20 companies. But more importantly, people began listening differently—not just to others, but to themselves.

And that was the real legacy.

Because reflective leadership doesn't end with a title or a TED Talk. It lives in the everyday moments—a pause in a hallway, a brave conversation in a meeting, a question asked instead of a command issued.

It's in the leaders who choose to mirror before they manage. Who choose presence before performance. Who choose to listen... before they lead.

So wherever you are—on a stage, in a boardroom, or at your kitchen table—pause.

**Reflect.**

**And lead.**

*"The better you listen, the stronger you lead. And the stronger you lead... the better you live."*

*Author's Note: If this story resonated with you, share it with someone who leads—or wants to. Reflective leadership is a movement, and it begins with a single, intentional pause.*

Dr. R Harrison Baxter

Contact:

info@rharrisonbaxter.com

www.linkedin.com/in/rharrisonbaxter

www.thelistentoleadsuite.com

https://calendly.com/meetrharrison/reflective-leadership-workshops

# Jessa Packard

My mission is to remind you that you are not broken. You are more than enough exactly as you are, and meant to thrive. I know this because I've been right where you are

I went from living on a millionaire's income to waiting in line at a diaper bank because diapers were more than I could afford. I was scared, stressed, and drowning in debt. Overnight, I became solely responsible for my boys—one three-year-old and I a baby. For the first time in my life, I was mentally and financially destitute—two things that nearly took me out. Everything that happened left me doubting myself and in constant fear and anxiety.

I knew there had to be more. In a world that felt out of my control, I chose to begin focusing on the one thing I could control—myself.

As I started embracing different healing modalities, I began noticing something—so many people, just like me, were stuck. They were searching for happiness, love, and freedom, but they were consumed by anxiety, fear, and self-doubt, just trying to survive. That's not how we're meant to live. We're meant to thrive, laugh, and experience real joy.

I want to guide you toward being courageous in trusting yourself again, embracing your worth, and loving every part of your story—no matter how messy it feels. When we stop hiding, we begin to step into our true power. It's time to build the confidence to stand tall and unlock the power already inside you

# Some Dates Never Leave You

## *By Jessa Packard*

Some dates tattoo themselves into your memory, forever etched in your mind, impossible to forget. If you lived through 9/11, you remember exactly where you were, what you were doing, and how it felt to witness the world change in an instant.

For me, the date August 22, 2021 holds that same power.

I woke up that morning, staring at the ceiling, unsure if I was still trapped in a nightmare. But I wasn't. The nightmare was real. My baby was screaming in his crib, but I couldn't move. I was numb. The weight of what had happened in the days before paralyzed me. I don't know how long I laid there.

All I know is that it took my three-year-old tugging on my arm, crying that he was hungry, to get me out of bed. No matter how broken I felt, my kids still needed me. The details leading up to that day don't matter. What matters is that it changed me on a level I never saw coming—physically, emotionally, and mentally.

For years after, I wished I could go back to the girl I was before everything wrecked me—the one who didn't overthink everything, who didn't carry constant heaviness in her chest or battle depression that swallowed her confidence and self-trust. That girl believed in herself. She tried things. She was brave. But she felt gone—and on top of everything else, I carried so much shame that I couldn't get back to her.

August 22, 2021, wasn't the worst day of my life. It was the start of two of the darkest, most excruciating years I've ever lived. The trauma didn't just live in my mind—it took root in my body. Fear and anxiety stopped being occasional visitors and became full-time tenants. On the outside, I still looked like me—smiling, cracking jokes—but inside, I was mentally shattered, financially drowning, barely keeping my head above water... and terrified that life would finally drag me under.

Every day felt like survival on repeat. Bills. Debt. Anxiety that even medication couldn't touch. Sleepless nights followed by mornings I didn't want to face. Things like laundry, making dinner, or answering a text feel like mountains I'd never summit. I was surviving while carrying the crushing weight of knowing two little boys needed me to do more than just survive.

By August 2023, almost two years had passed. I had mastered the act—smile when expected, say "I'm good" when asked, keep it light. But behind the scenes, I was exhausted. Still stuck in the same cycles: people-pleasing, chasing validation, I was fine when I wasn't.

I tried everything—therapy, journaling, affirmations, morning routines. Everyone said, "Change your thoughts, change your life," so I did. But nothing changed.

Eventually, I started to believe I was the problem. I wondered what was wrong with me. I envied the women who faced similar battles and came out stronger, braver—thriving. That wasn't me. I was frozen in fear.

That kind of thinking is a dangerous trap. Especially when you've made choices you regret—like I had. When you've been in relationships that made you question everything about yourself. The kind that slowly breaks you down in silence, making you feel like too much and not enough all at once.

That kind of confusion isn't just painful. It's lonely.

**The Call That Changed Everything**

September 2023, I got a call that stopped everything. The doctor had found something. "We think it might be cancer. We need more tests." I hung up, breathless. *What happens to my kids if I'm gone—or too sick to care for them?*

That week, something in me shifted. I realized no one was coming to save me. I had clung to the victim role, believing I was trying—but deep down, I wasn't facing the truth. My problem wasn't effort. It was avoidance.

I had a choice: *Could I build a life I wanted—even if it looked different from the one I lost?* That idea felt huge and overwhelming.

So I asked myself: *Which doors are closed? Which ones are open and waiting for me?*

The one I was clinging to was shut—with caution tape across it. But I kept begging, *Please open. Please stop hurting me so I can walk through you.* Deep down, I knew—it never would. Looking back was only hurting me.

That moment changed everything.

I threw myself into nervous system research and found a trauma expert training coaches. I didn't have the money, but I wrote down 30 names. People I could ask for a loan, promising to pay them back—with interest.

Two days later, I had $12,000.

I hired a coach and got certified in trauma-informed nervous system work. That's when it clicked—it wasn't about thinking positive or saying the right things. It was about giving my body what it actually needed: *safety.*

Once I started coaching others, I saw it everywhere. People weren't living; they were surviving. They kept getting knocked down, unsure why they couldn't reach the life they dreamed of. Some wanted more but didn't know how to get there, while others sabotaged their goals, not feeling safe to thrive.

They were just like me. It broke my heart to see so many stuck in the same patterns—trapped, confused, longing for peace but caught in pain. Not because they weren't trying, but because they didn't understand what was holding them back.

Too many live to please others, losing themselves little by little. It's no wonder the world feels so exhausting and overwhelming.

That's when my mission became clear: I had to help people—not just tell them they could thrive but show them how. Step by step. In a way their nervous systems could handle, so change could stick. So, they could experience true fulfillment, purpose, and peace.

Above all, I wanted to remind people:

You are not too broken.

You are not behind.

You are not the victim.

You are the hero.

You've *always* been the hero.

You just forgot.

So, let's walk through the door that's already open—and waiting for you.

**The badges we wear**

I know what it's like to spend years breaking patterns, rewriting stories you never asked for, and carrying pain you didn't choose but still have to heal from. Some days, pausing to breathe instead of reacting feels like a win. Some nights, choosing vulnerability over shutting down feels like a miracle.

I wasn't always the woman I am today. I used to crave passion, adventure, and a partner who'd meet me there. But I kept choosing men who gave me flattery and chaos—never safety. I yelled when I was hurting. I said things like, "Maybe we should just get divorced," not because I meant them, but because I was too scared to ask for what I needed. I tested people to see if they'd stay. It felt automatic—like I couldn't stop.

That's what emotional programming does. It takes over when you're scared, hurt, or vulnerable. And unless you know how to rewire it, you stay stuck in the same cycles. I see it all the time—with clients, friends, even strangers. We start with an idea for our futures—how it's "supposed" to look. But then something crashes. The relationship ends. The job disappears. The dream dies. And instead of adjusting, we cling even harder—not to what *is*, but to what should've been.

That's an attachment. And it keeps us stuck. Ironically, the dream you're holding onto so tightly starts to sabotage you. It blocks your healing, your growth, your peace. Because you're clinging to a fantasy—and missing what's real. That's how we end up in draining relationships, soul-numbing jobs, and cycles that make us small. All while life is trying to hand us something better—but we're too afraid to let go and receive it.

After the relationship ends, after the business fails, even after the dream clearly dies—we still hold on. Not because it fits anymore, but because we wanted it so badly. The problem isn't you; it's the power you've given to everything outside of you. The meaning you've attached to other people's behavior. The way you've let those experiences define your identity.

We all do it. Someone's cold or distant with you. Suddenly your mind spins: Did I do something wrong? Am I not enough? Maybe they're drowning in something you can't see. Still, you make it about you.

It doesn't stop there. You get laid off, and suddenly you feel like you're not good enough. A family member betrays you, and you believe you're not worthy of loyalty. A miscarriage, a cheating spouse, or a heartbreak you didn't see coming makes you think you're unlovable. Somewhere along the way, it all becomes part of your identity.

Your brain, wired to find patterns, starts feeding you lies to make sense of the pain. These lies don't just float through your mind; they root themselves deep, becoming your inner dialogue, your default settings, the lens through which you see the world. Unless you interrupt them, they keep running your life. That's why the same pain, wounds, and situations keep resurfacing.

Before long, you're convinced you're the problem. But you're not. You've just been living in a story that was never yours to carry. We all grew up in systems—religious, cultural, familial—taught who we were supposed to be. We sought answers outside of ourselves: from parents, teachers, leaders. In trying to meet their expectations, we lost connection with the only voice that truly matters—our own.

As the world gets louder, your intuition gets drowned out. Eventually, your inner voice fades... until one day, you don't recognize yourself.

Maybe you're still reading because you feel stuck. Deep down, you know there's more—but you don't know where to start. Maybe you keep attracting relationships that leave you drained. Maybe you hear people talk about "loving yourself" or "being authentic," but you're not sure how to get there.

Here's the truth: You're not broken. You're buried. And the moment you start peeling back the layers, letting go of the noise, and releasing what was never really you—that's when you'll meet the real you. The one who's been there all along.

### Here's a truth I'm certain of

Coincidences aren't random. Not even close. What we call "coincidences" are really nudges from God, the Universe—whatever you believe in—trying to guide you forward. They are proof you're not alone. You are not lost. And you *are* moving forward, even if it doesn't feel like it yet. These nudges are little reminders to keep going.

So if you're reading this right now? It's not by accident. There's a reason you're here *at this* moment, reading these words—whether or not you've heard of me before—trust it.

During the times when nothing seems to be happening—or worse, when it feels like everything is falling apart—it's hard to believe you're on the right path. I couldn't. Things falling apart or not working out the way you imagined happen for a reason. God, the Universe, is trying to hand you something better, but you're too afraid to let go and receive it.

Now let's talk about a phrase we hear all the time: **"Just let go"**.

Let go of *them*.

Let go of *the past*.

Let go of *the business that didn't work out*.

Yeah, easier said than done. You can't force yourself to let go. You can't bully yourself into healing. Your body—your nervous system—holds on to what's hurt you. It remembers. Its not weakness. It's neuroscience.

So instead of forcing it, I teach something different—because letting go didn't seem possible for me. I said I wanted to, but the truth is, I wanted to *want* to let go. I wanted to feel free. I wanted to start living again, despite everything. But some part of me was still holding on. That's how the 'Open Door Theory' was born—a way to focus on doing the next right thing. It felt too simple at first, but slowly, it pulled me out of my own inner rat race. When I shared it with others and they began to feel real relief, I realized it wasn't just a personal coping strategy. It was something bigger—something that could help my friends, my clients, and maybe even you.

Later, I found out *neurologically*, it made perfect sense. When your nervous system has been in survival mode for too long, even the smallest decisions—like what to eat or where to go—can feel paralyzing.

You freeze. You second guess. You ask others what you should do. Why? Because somewhere along the way, you stopped trusting yourself. You became terrified of making the "wrong" choice. So you stay in a loop of indecision, anxiety, overwhelm, and self-doubt. I know that cycle well because I've lived it.

When you've been hurt, it's natural to crave control. You think: *If I can just plan enough, I won't get blindsided again.* So, you map out every possible outcome, play out your entire future before it even happens, and cling tightly to anything that feels certain.

But life doesn't work like that. And trying to force it only feeds the anxiety. So here's the mindset shift: stop trying to plan 100 steps ahead. Start with the next best decision. And before that return to one powerful step—accept what's happened.

This doesn't mean you approve of it, are okay with what someone did to you, excuse their behavior, or minimize your pain. It simply means you're no longer pretending it didn't happen. Because as long as you're bargaining with the past, wishing things were different, playing the "what if" game, or holding onto hope that someone will finally change, you're keeping yourself stuck in a version of life that isn't real.

**The Open Door Theory**

Imagine your life like a hallway filled with doors. Some are shut, some locked. Some are cracked open, others wide open. Too often, we stand in front of the closed ones—banging, crying, begging someone to open them back up. We try to force our way in simply because it's familiar. We tell ourselves, *If I can just get this door open again, everything will be alright.*

Sometimes, we even walk through the slightly cracked ones—ignoring the ones flung wide open for us.

How often do we bang on a closed door, finally walk back through it, and then wonder why it's so difficult? The sooner we can lovingly walk away from what's closed—and stop settling for what's barely cracked open—the sooner we can step into what's fully available to us.

Does that mean a closed door will never open again? Maybe. But for now—it's not. And if it's not open right now, don't pause your life waiting for it to be. Instead, pause. Hold yourself. Validate that it hurts. And then… look around and move.

What doors are open? What's right in front of you, waiting for you to step toward it? You don't have to sprint or know exactly where it leads. Take one step, pause, look around, learn, try, and give it your all—then adjust if needed.

That's how you move forward. One door, one step, one moment at a time.

And with every step, life will bring more love & clarity. What I'm sharing isn't magic—it's a process. And I'm here to walk you through it.

**First: Power of your breath:**

Your body needs oxygen not only to survive but to shift from fight-or-flight mode to a calm, safe state. This calm state is necessary for healing and moving forward.

I use the 4-5-6 breathing method with every client, my kids, and myself when I feel overwhelmed:

- Inhale for 4 counts
- Hold for 5 counts
- Exhale for 6 counts

Repeat five times. The slow exhale delivers oxygen faster than traditional breathing. Treat yourself as you would a scared child. You wouldn't yell or blame them, yet we do that to ourselves. We expect to bounce back instantly.

Instead, speak kindly to yourself:

- "You're safe."
- "You're strong."
- "You're worthy of love and being seen."

We weren't taught to be kind to ourselves. Instead, we were told to "just be happy." So, offer yourself the same compassion you'd give a hurting child.

**Second: Clear Vision**

What do you really want your life to look like? Be honest. Not the watered-down version that fits your current reality—but the one that lights you up. The life you've barely let yourself dream of because it feels too far away.

Let yourself go there.

What brings you joy, peace, excitement? Do you see yourself in a cozy mountain home or near the beach? Taking seasonal vacations? Working just a few hours a week doing something you love?

It might feel unrealistic—but this is how many have created the lives they once only dreamed about. It starts with permission. With writing it down. And with believing it's possible.

**Third: Safe surroundings**

It took me a long time to learn this: not everyone deserves access to your energy. Be intentional with who you let close. Surround yourself with people who support, love, and celebrate you—the ones who see your worth and reflect it back.

If someone constantly makes you feel anxious, small, or like you're walking on eggshells, that's not just in your head. That's your nervous system signaling something's off. Listen. Be honest about who uplifts you and who drains you. You can't heal until you feel safe.

DM me "safe circle" on Instagram @jessapackard, for a powerful tool I teach to help you with this

## Fourth: Self-Acceptance

You've heard: "Healing takes time," "Be patient." While that's partly true, healing doesn't have to take forever. It starts the moment you choose something different. The moment you stop trying to fix yourself and start accepting who you are, right now.

What keeps most people stuck is resistance—resisting emotions, judging them, trying to push them away. That resistance sends a message to your brain: "This is dangerous." Your body responds by locking up, bracing itself, and keeping the cycle alive.

But emotions are just energy in motion. They're meant to move—if you let them. Give your feelings space without shame, labels, or the urge to solve them. That's where freedom begins.

Acceptance doesn't mean giving up. It means saying, "This is how I feel right now... and I still get to want more." Resignation says, "Nothing can change." But acceptance? Acceptance is power. It's choosing to feel your pain and still move forward. It's choosing love, presence, and possibility—right here, as you are.

Because you are.

## Fifth: Consistency

After trauma, your nervous system shifts into survival mode. You stop choosing from peace and start choosing from fear, protection, and scarcity. That's why nervous system regulation is essential—it's not just a mindset, it's *body-set.*

Your nervous system connects your brain to your heart, gut, lungs, muscles, and skin. At the center is the vagus nerve, constantly asking, *"Am I safe?"* When regulated, you feel calm and connected. When dysregulated, it feels like there's an alarm going off inside—even if there's no real threat. The past lives on in your body.

Think of it like this: you take the same route every day. One day, you're forced onto a detour—more peaceful, more scenic. But as soon as the old road reopens, you go back to it. Not because it's better, but because it's familiar. That's how patterns form. People repeat cycles—not because they're broken—but because their nervous system is wired that way.

And here's the key: your brain doesn't know the difference between a story you tell it and reality. Every thought, behavior, or reaction strengthens that wiring. The cycle continues—unless you interrupt it and consistently choose something different. How, start small. Ask yourself, *"What would my future self choose right now?"* Then do that. One conscious choice at a time creates new pathways. Over time, your brain begins to these new nerve pathways and you dont repeat old patterns.

**The magic of the Open Door Theory:**

Remember, every open door brings something with it—growth, clarity, a lesson, a healing, a relationship, a breakthrough. Whatever it is, it's meant for you.

As you continue walking through open doors, something powerful happens—you begin to trust yourself again. Not because you have all the answers, but because you're learning to move forward into the unknown with certainty everything is working out. You're learning to choose yourself, stay present, and to give everything you have to each new experience—without regret

Sometimes, only one door will be open. You'll know it's the one. Other times, you'll face multiple options. Release the need to know the right answer. Whether the door was "right" or "wrong", it still gives you valuable data. If it's not aligned, you gain clarity. If it is, it is even better. Both situations you learned. That's how real confidence is built—not from perfection, but from movement.

So if you're facing a closed door right now, here's what I want you to remember: You don't need to know what's next. Just find the next open door. If it's open, trust that it's for you. You don't need to fully understand it—just walk through it.

If there are several open doors, ask: Which one feels the most aligned? Trust what comes up. Make a decision. Sit with it if you need to. If it's not meant for you, you'll feel it. If it is, you'll grow into it. Remember the need to control every outcome stems from fear and change is the one thing you can always count on. With every change comes a new opportunity—to grow, to align, to discover more of who you really are.

The Open Door Theory isn't about predicting the future. It's about choosing to move—one present, brave step at a time—back to the truest, rawest version of you. The version you love and trust.

\*\*\*

To contact Jessa:

Instagram: @Jessapackard or @lifestylewithjessa

Tik tok: @jessapackard

YouTube: @jpcoaching

Website: JESSAPACKARD.com

Facebook: Jessa Packard

Email: info@jessapackard.com

# Antomius Wise

Antomius Wise is an experienced Life Coach, Business Mentor, Tax Guru, and Relationship Expert based in Virginia, Maryland, and Washington, D.C. (DMV), offering life strategies around the globe. With a high-value mindset, he is a solution-based thinker who is pro-truth.

With over ten years of experience in the nonprofit and finance industries, Antomius has overcome countless obstacles to get where he is today. His clients are professional athletes, high-ranking officials, business executives, and everyday people seeking advice and guidance.

He was a professional athlete in the NFL, obtained an MBA, started an asset protection business that his family operates, and founded a 501(C)(3) that supports domestic violence situations. He has Federal Law Enforcement experience with the United States Secret Service, found a woman willing to be a helpmate and allows him to be great, produced two sons, and assisted many clients in obtaining their ultimate goals. His life is fulfilled, and the biggest reward is bringing value to society and creating economic growth.

Why does he do this? It is his way of bringing value to society. As a Life Strategist, he volunteers his time, experience, knowledge, guidance, and understanding to Wise Protective Services and More, Inc. (501(c)(3), to raise money and awareness for domestic violence victims (mental and physical). 100% of the proceeds go to WPSM.org. That means it's all a tax deduction!!

# Intro to Life_Strategies_2.0

## *By Antomius Wise*

**"The key to patience is doing something in the meantime."**

I would like you to close your eyes and think about this for a moment. Have you ever wondered what to do after you set your goals? Goals don't come to fruition overnight. I came up with a quote to give you peace of mind and embrace monotony while you're on the journey. "The key to patience is doing something in the meantime!"

Hi, my name is Antomius Wise. Providing solutions and bringing value to society has always been important to me. I have achieved everything I had envisioned up to this point because of this approach. I understand and value what it is to be "in the moment." This philosophy allowed me to decrease my chances of bad things happening to me at an early age, assisting me into adulthood to make logical decisions and allowing me to communicate with you today.

I started my journey as a Life Strategist in 2016. Getting there was more than just accomplishing goals, overcoming adversity, and some internal doubt. The question was whether I was ready to advise someone on how to fish, rather than just give them a fish, so that they can achieve their desired outcomes on their life journey.

Learning how to bring value to society and using your abilities to bring your vision to fruition are two key components that I will touch on. Understanding this gave me the ability to excel during the journey of life while also assisting others along my journey. I'm proof that these concepts can give you the fuel and ammunition to overcome any obstacles you could face. With these critical components, I positioned myself to have conversations with many of our Presidents and other notable people in the world. I found that we all had this one "major" thing in common-can you guess what that was? Keep reading to find out what happens next. Every topic I discuss below has a course. I only cover topics I have first-hand experience with. After all, experience is the best teacher.

## Professional Athlete: The three phases to go from nothing to something

As a 5-year-old kid, I promised my mom that I was going to go to the NFL. She passed away three years later. Soon after, I started to set my life up to keep that promise to my mother and accomplish the goal of making it to the NFL. As I grew, I realized that navigating this path would be challenging. So, I adopted three phases to help me along the way. Those three principal pillars were **imagination, faith, and discipline**.

**Imagination** is one of the most powerful tools that the Most High blessed any of us with. It's the beginning of creating all new things. There were many days I would imagine myself playing in front of thousands of people, being looked at in a Godly way, or just getting paid handsomely for something I love to do. For this to all take shape, I had to have the imagination and plant the seed so that my ideas and dreams would flourish.

When you have **faith**, anything is possible. And without it, nothing is possible. There were many times people would tell me to give up on my dream of making it to the NFL. They would say things like "just graduate from college, don't worry about the NFL," "you're too big to play CB (cornerback)," and the most famous one was "fewer than 2% of college football players will get an opportunity to go to the NFL". These are just some things they would say and laugh in my face about. I switched from my imagination phase to my faith phase very quickly. I always said to myself, "as long as I have breath in my body, I have a chance." When you have faith, it's similar to having a secret generator only you know about. For it to be activated, you must connect it to your imagination. If it's not connected, you have nothing, no power, no fuel, etc. Faith gives you the opportunity from within, which means you have to make opportunities yourself.

**Discipline** requires putting in the work while still applying faith and imagination. I went to four colleges to give myself a better opportunity to advance to the NFL. Michael Strahan, Jay Glazier, and many others in the NFL circles called me "4-schools" because I actually went to four different colleges to make this opportunity happen. Coming up on possibly my last year of college eligibility for football, I knew this could be my last shot. My imagination and faiths were all at the forefront, and this was when discipline kicked in. I made it through the season with good evaluations from NFL Scouts. Many of them projected I would be a late-round pick if I stayed in school for my last year of eligibility, per NAIA approval. My eligibility was denied. My imagination, faith, and discipline allowed me to stay focused and bring the NFL vision to fruition. My life consisted of cold calling/networking with NFL scouts to keep my name on their radar, working out sprinting with 45-pound-sleds, doing intense plyometrics five days a week, and operating a forklift loading tiles on trucks since I needed money. NFL Pro Day came, and things went great. On draft day I got the opportunity to go to the NFL's Washington Redskins (now Washington Commanders).

Applying the three principles put me in a position to go from nothing to something. Always remember, "The key to patience is to do something in the meantime."

**Entrepreneur mindset: Stepping on good to become great**

All of us have goals we'd like to achieve, but most dreams take time to come to fruition. You must live, function, and bring value to all facets of your life while you're on that path. This is what I call being patient while you strive towards your goals.

Setting a minor goal every day helps tremendously! Having an open mind to change something if it's ineffective is also key. You don't want to continue doing the same thing over and over if it's not working. That's insanity. It is sometimes necessary for us to put pride aside for a moment and be open to making changes to find a solution. Change the plan, not the dream.

While navigating life's journey, you will notice people content with being average. There's nothing wrong with that. It's their life, right? You will also see that some people are willing to recalibrate their minds, understand the power of networking. They are prepared to become a human sponge, sacrifice, find solutions and solve problems. These people are willing to step on good to become great.

Being cut from the NFL, watching your dreams unravel, can seem like death. Yes, I said DEATH. Being laid off as a W-2 employee during a crisis can appear that your world is crumbling at your fingertips. What do you do when the opportunity is nowhere in sight? You create it.

**Building a solid foundation: Spirituality, financially and in relationships**

During my time on and off of NFL teams, I flirted with becoming an entrepreneur. When my football days were over, the time for flirting ended, and it was time to commit to building a kingdom. Spirituality, finances, and relationships all play an integral role in building a kingdom in modern times.

I started studying the scriptures, our western civilization, and the money system. That's when I found out the truth about society - navigating your way through the corporate world is not the end all be all. It's owning your own kingdom and being personally debt-free. When you understand our society from a macrocosmic standpoint, it assists you with becoming a solution-based thinker, opens you up to having a ruling class king mentality.

The entrepreneur journey took off by recalibrating my mind. As you recalibrate your mind, you will need to let go of many things' society instilled in you as a child. You have to be willing to go on a journey to obtain new information, seek successful mentors, apply the information learned, and look to improve what society has already created. When you can create something new, solve problems and provide solutions, society will reward you. It allows you to be your own boss.

I started an asset protection company, protecting celebrities and hedge fund managers. People will always need protection no matter where they are in the world. If there is a need, you provide a solution. Things were good, but I wanted them to be great. I had to ask myself, "What distinguishes me from other companies?" This question led me to recognize that I needed a solid credential to be taken seriously. So, I put myself in a position to join the United States Secret Service. The naysayers would say that I put the cart before the horse. I say that I just put a motor in the cart and put the horse in the stable.

During this time, my protection business is doing well, and I'm going through the process for the position with the Secret Service until a hiring freeze occurs. As my motto goes, "The key to patience is doing something in the meantime," so I had to keep things moving. I noticed that the tax code is structured so that if you're bringing value to society, then the government will reward you. Being a three-dimensional thinker and at times four-dimensional on some spiritual knowledge, I saw a need in my community and immediately set up a 501(c)(3) nonprofit to assist domestic violence situations. At this point, I'm moving into the High-Value Man category. The trajectory is through the roof and beyond. I finally got the call from the Secret Service, and I proudly accepted it.

**High-Value Relationships**

If you have a good grasp of the scriptures as a man who understands how to protect, provide, prophesy, and preach, you increase your chances of a High-Value woman coming your way. Speaking from experience, I chose one for marriage. I designed courses for these types of relationships. Let's be honest; no one wants to go through life's journey alone.

This portion pertains to people who have or strive to have means. For those who desire to get married possibly, this is one of the most significant investments you will make. Example: If you're earning a million dollars, and your spouse decides to exercise the option of "irreconcilable differences" that's half gone from your pocket; let's not forget about taxes - another 30-40%, you're close to $200K, yikes. I'm not here to discourage anyone from marriage; I'm here to increase your chances of possible solutions to reach your desired outcomes. While you are on your way, I will provide you with a few strategies to think about.

**For Married Couples: Bringing value to your relationship**

During and since the Covid-19 pandemic, people's thoughts were often centered around their relationship status. Some couples had to be around each other 24 hours a day throughout the quarantine period. Some realized how much they needed each other, and some realized the opposite.

A lot of people believe that love is the foundation of marriage. This isn't a fairy tale. In reality, you should consider that you are together for "duty" to one another. Knowing what value you can bring to the relationship and whether that aligns with your partner's philosophy is paramount. Understanding how to embrace monotony, repetition, and sacrifice increases your chances of a healthy marriage.

Former POTUS John F. Kennedy, Jr. said it best, "Ask not what your country can do for you–ask what you can do for your country." Make sure you give 110% in all aspects of your life and show the value you can add. If the relationship ends, you won't have any regrets. Nothing is more frustrating than the "should've, could've, would've" feeling. Time waits for no one. We all get 24 hours in a day. What are you doing with yours?

## For Men: How to obtain and maintain a ruling class mentality

I've had many conversations with a number of highly influential people across the world, and I'd like to share a few components that define a high-value man. Financial resources, recognition by other high-value men (HVM), being part of a network of high-value men, visibility, utility, discernment, integrity, ethics, discipline, and morals define a High-Value Man (HVM). I don't make the rules of society. I just understand how to apply, use and teach them to you so you can find solutions to reach your desired outcomes.

This course is specifically for those men who have or are open to having a ruling class king mentality. I use the term "open" because many men may not be as well-read of the scriptures to know of the gifts that the most-high stored upon them to understand female nature.

For those with discernment and knowledge to use those gifts, strategies can be implemented to advise you on the tax codes. I will also discuss ways to protect your assets before getting married so that you don't get taken behind the shed by the courts doing what they please to you if you get divorced.

There are also strategies for those that are already married. Since most women today are considered "modern," knowing what laws and tax codes benefit you in modern times is essential.

For those that don't know about these gifts yet but are willing to learn, there are strategies for you as well. To obtain this level of knowledge, you must be ready to come in good faith and make things happen. This will be the beginning stage on your way to creating wealth. The strategies outlined are very solution focused.

You can still be solution-based and married, but you must structure your kingdom to deal with people/relationships from a position of power.

**For Women: Be his peace and be his paradise**

This course is specifically for women who want to be chosen for marriage or a long-term relationship by High-Value Men (HVM). In most of my consultations with women, they seldom describe the average guy when it comes to what type of man they would like when chosen for marriage. They'll have this idea of some "mythical man" who is considered wealthy, handsome, athletic, corporate, street, godly, and a little bit of a bad boy. So, I had to develop a series of questions to increase their chances of finding solutions to reach their desired outcomes. The one question that seems to perplex them is, "Do you know what these HVM look for and value in a woman so you can have the opportunity to be selected for marriage by them?" Remember, many times, the men ask will you marry me and the women can choose to accept. The keyword is "opportunity" and my course is like having a study guide to the final exam.

The pandemic gave many ladies a taste of what it would be like to be living alone, with a dog/cat without the access of a man, and thoughts of possibly dying alone. Let's just say it didn't feel good. Having a 501(c)(3) that assists domestic violence situations, many ladies wanted to pick my brain during consultations about how to increase their chances and opportunities to get this type of man.

Once you've passed the initial attractive stage, the number one thing you must do to give yourself this opportunity is to provide him with peace of mind. A man of this type is a protector and a provider. He is someone who is driven, working up to 16 hours a day, and is looking for peace.

Every woman isn't going to get a professional athlete, entertainer, or wealthy guru to marry them. There are men in the middle making six figures, on their purpose, and have the ability to put a woman in a position to have the "option" if she wants to work. The media doesn't advertise these men as much because "allegedly" in the late '60s, it is believed that society could make more money off of women if she is not within a good covenant of a man.

Many modern women aren't focusing on getting married and being a wife in early adulthood. That's ok. Some strategies can be implemented and executed to increase your chances of obtaining your desired outcomes with these particular men. We are in the age of information, and for ladies who want to live this type of lifestyle, you do something about it.

## Corporate Marriages: Looking good together

Everyone involved knows this is a business. Both parties would sit down; consult about their duties and expectations for the marriage. These marriages typically are for financially successful individuals who like their own space. These couples usually have scheduled get-togethers, events, family gatherings. Let's face it, not too many people want to go through life alone. This option gives them the best of both worlds.

## Final thoughts:

As a life strategist, I will assist you with understanding society from a macrocosmic standpoint and how to bring value. Together, we will expand your mental agility, so that you will be able to reach your desired outcomes. I'm primarily based in the DC area, and offer phone consultations and virtual sessions. One-on-one, couples, group sessions, and speaking engagements are available.

Throughout my story, strategies from my courses were utilized in my life to gain optimal results. Some other courses we offer are a 501(c)(3) finance course to create wealth, consultations on mindset, motivation, and many others that are designed to assist you in solving problems as well as achieving your goals.

Life is a long journey, and tomorrow is not promised to any of us. We all get 24 hours in a day. What are you doing with yours?

**Quote "The key to patience is doing something in the meantime."**

**Attribute - Antomius Wise**

To contact Antomius:

Experienced Life Coach, Business Mentor, Tax Guru, and Relationship Expert

Pro-truth / Solution-based thinker / High-Value Mindset

Based in Virginia, Maryland, and Washington, D.C. (DMV)

Life_Strategies_2.0: lifestrategies20.com

Wise Protective Service and More, INC.: wpsm.org

Wise Protective Services, LLC: Wiseprotectiveservices.com

***

► **LET'S CONNECT:**

Book a consult: lifestrategies20.com/lets-connect

Phone: 678-568-6092

Email: AWise.LifeStrategies2.0@gmail.com

LinkedIn: @Life_Strategies_2.0

FB: @Life_Strategies_2.0

IG: @life_stratgies_2.0

Twitter: @LifeStrat20

TikTok: @lifestrategies2.0

Pinterest: @LifeStrategies2point0

Reddit: https://www.reddit.com/user/AntomiusWise

Patreon: https://www.patreon.com/LifeStrategies20

YouTube: https://www.youtube.com/user/awise5405

# Brad Balfour

Born in Youngstown, Ohio, Brad Balfour's parents moved to Cincinnati in 1960 or '61. With that move, he immersed himself in collecting comic books, trading cards, toys and more. Unlike his peers, he somehow realized he should save all this pop culture detritus. Thus, a pack-rat archivist was born.

Though he never expected to be a wordsmith, Balfour began writing in junior high school. While he wasn't going to be a lawyer or a doctor (as his dad wished), he was planning to be a Rabbi until, at 18, he landed the editor's job at the Queen's Jester, Cincy's alternative paper. He moved on to be the Cincinnati Post's rock critic in 1975. He never looked back from there as he moved to NYC and a series of cool editorial gigs.

Once he hit the Big Apple, Balfour's life went from local to international, from music to film and every other kind of pop culture possibility as he wrote interviews, reviews, and commentary in print, online, video and live. He even scripted a graphic novel/screenplay with noted author John Shirley. For the next 45 years he racked up an impressive array of experiences.

From interviewing Steve Jobs (for the Apple Store NYC debut), shaking hands with President Bill Clinton after Nelson Mandela's speech inaugurating the Tribeca Film Festival, to working on articles in Heavy Metal with Stephen King and William Burroughs, he's had enough experiences to fill several volumes. His interviews and writings have been included in several books and international publications.

Balfour continues to produce stories weekly, reaching an audience of thousands — maybe millions — through his multiple online outlets. Right now, he's in talks to transform his archives into a docu-series, podcast and various publications.

# Finding Identity Through Memoir: Creating A Life Story Worthy for Others to Read

## *By Brad Balfour*

For years I grappled with the idea of writing a memoir. Though it's a slice of a life, a memoir needs to be more than that. It should have a theme, rationale and purpose whether as a warning, inspiration or declaration.

I've been asked to edit memoirs, ghostwrite them or even obtain the contents from conversations with my client. But when I was hired to draw the fascinating details out of a man turning 100, the challenge of creating his memoir upped my game. Thankfully he had an uncanny memory, spewing out details beyond expectation. But the project also posed an entangled set of complications.

My client was a World War II vet and a political activist, deeply involved with his synagogue. Also, a fine art publisher and an art appraiser dealing with controversial works. Though he'd led a fascinating life, fashioning a memoir out of that proved to be quite a task. Not only did I need details — dates, locations and people's names — to correctly sequence, I had to determine which points needed emphasis and elaboration versus other content that would best be underplayed.

In doing so, I had to negotiate between what I thought made sense, what my client most cared about and, ultimately, what his overbearing wife thought should be done regardless of my suggestions. The project never became the story I thought it should have been. Though I was paid some of what we agreed on, she did what I thought she'd ultimately do — adopt my suggestions without letting me finish, thus depriving me both of credit for the work and the final payment for it.

I learned two things from that experience. First to know when and how to define parameters. Next, write a contract that takes into account such ambiguous variables.

More importantly, I absorbed crucial lessons for making an effective memoir… or not.

I needed to discover my own story and what made it come together. Who was I? Was there a mission in my life and what words would I share?

Recently, I was sent a memoir written by a friend's cousin. His story was one of survival, having landed in prison. He did a pretty good job of capturing his state of mind and how he'd managed to get things together enough to write more than 20,000 words.

I asked, "Besides helping you order your past and discover your motivating focus -- is this a way to know whether or not you have a worthy story to tell? Why did you need to write a memoir?

"If you want to have a full-blown memoir, it needs to be more than just a chronology and a description of your emotional states. Besides examining what's happened and the emotions behind your life's events, you need to develop your story more visually and narratively. It needs descriptions. What did that building look like? What was notable about its location?

"You've lived your life, but now you need to help your audience feel what it was like to do that."

I then decided to craft a memoir for myself and have begun with no urgent deadline. What would I consider worthy of inclusion in a memoir of my own making?

Although surviving in New York City without collapsing into drug addiction, suicide or madness might be considered worthy of a memoir on its own merits, that's not the case here. I had to discover my deeper story and understand why it made sense. It had to come together as more than just a factual rendition, conveying a deeper, driving mission.

My story isn't so much about a struggle against adversity, but about being a witness and an advocate -- of cutting-edge culture. As a journalist who's interviewed celebrities for decades, I've seen a world of shifting sensibilities and the growth of a global pop culture.

We all start out as part of our local village culture — our neighborhood or whatever ethnic community we identify with. But we grow up to be part of a national culture we connect to.

Transcending all that is the international pop culture which unifies us globally — much of it thanks to the shared "reality" of the internet and social media. Connecting with what gets called cool, hip progressive, avant-garde, it means embracing whatever disrupts the conventional day-to-day humdrum existence.

As far back as I can remember, I was a disruptive child. Why? I don't know. But I went from merely disruptive to being a socially constructive disruptor after discovering MEDIA. I consumed anything in newspapers — especially if about science, music and pop culture.

I began reading at an early age (maybe two or three years old), gobbling up books with stories about dinosaurs at first, then comic books and science fiction. In reading about science and history, I got to know stuff without being force-fed. My mother always said she was lucky -- blessed by the fact that she could sit me in a corner and stick a book in my hand. I'd then stay quietly engrossed in whatever she had provided.

Born in Youngstown, a gray-hued industrial city in Northeastern Ohio, my earliest memories somehow tied in with the things that would later become core to my life. The first few songs I recalled were Elvis Presley's classic "Hound Dog" — because I identified with a hot dog stand in the form of a big dog — and Johnny Cash's intense 1963 "Ring of Fire."

I was fascinated by astronauts and collected clippings about them. Leaving the planet seemed like an exciting idea, so TV programs such as "The Twilight Zone," "The Outer Limits" and "Star Trek" were revelatory. Among the many comics I discovered were superhero favorites such as Silver Age Green Lantern, The Flash, Spiderman, The Fantastic Four among the many others.

When I was about five years old, we moved to Cincinnati — on Newfield, part of Bond Hill, a neighborhood that was once Jewish and was becoming ethnically mixed at the time. Even when I was five, I was a disruptor. My mom explained that kids got mad when I knew all the answers and blurted them out without raising my hand.

Around six years old, I made it my mission to both build a serious comic book collection and, eventually, have my own small museum in the basement. A huge science nerd, I collected clippings of animals along with some actual animals themselves. Every Saturday, I went to the local Natural History Museum to hear the head curator teach classes about nature. I had bug boxes, a real stuffed fox and lizard plus lots of rocks and shells. I put them all on display and cajoled other kids in helping me organize It — all at eight years old.

I explored all kinds of art in books and through an occasional museum visit. But when I discovered Dali and Magritte, such disruptive stuff fascinated me. Surrcalism, dada, abstract expressionism, pop art, minimalism, conceptual and performance art — I loved anything which challenged conventional notions of what defines art and makes it acceptable. Or not.

In elementary school, I had started drawing, inventing my own superhero characters and stories, gathered together in many notebooks. In fact, the first thing I professionally sold was a drawing for an underground newspaper.

But it was music that really charged my passions. My dad played jazz on LPs and 78s — Coleman Hawkins, Stan Kenton, Errol Garner, Sarah Vaughn and Ella Fitzgerald — and then I discovered progressive radio station WEBN and shows like Eclectic Stop Sign and Jazz & Poetry.

From free jazz to psychedelic rock, I was getting high without illegal drugs. Whether John Coltrane or Captain Beefheart was being played, my life was changed by rock n roll -- and more. The first single I bought, "The Israelites" by Desmond Dekker and The Aces wasn't Klezmer but Jamaican Rock Steady. My first five albums included Miles Davis' "Bitches Brew," Beefheart's "Lick My Decals Off, Baby," King Crimson's In The Court of The Crimson King" and The Flock's eponymous debut.

At that time, I became political. While Jewish social groups were shaping up, I was joining protest movements and socially concerned youth groups. Of course, being such an outlier, I got bullied which pushed me further into what local underground there was, hanging out at Kidd's bookstore talking about shows like "The Prisoner," Allen Ginsberg's poetry, Jack Kerouac's novels and the Velvet Underground's music.

# The Change[23]

When my mom found a clipping announcing an up-coming Midwestcon in 1967, I joined the original outlier crowd -- science fiction fandom. The original "cons" (conventions) that emerged in the '30s -- and have continued since -- led to all the fandoms that now populate comic-cons and such world-wide.

Ever since I discovered science fiction and sci-fi cons, I found a way to productively connect with outlier behavior. I launched my own mimeographed fanzine. Unlike the slick websites and Instagram pages one can create nowadays, these cheap print publications were made with crude stencils on ragged paper. I'm talking about a time when there were no Xerox machines or copiers, even cassette tapes.

With my fanzine, Diddy Wah Diddy, I merged proto-punk music commentary with sci-fi musings and grungy poetry aping the Beats (referencing beat poet Michael McClure). My identification with anti-mainstream, cutting edge, blood-on-the-tracks creators expanded.

Fast forward to my 16th year. I decided to be a rock critic. Hey, I could get free vinyl while joining other reprobates, degenerates and cranks. And thanks to my high school newspaper, The Bulldog Barks, I published my first reviews, that of "Lick My Decals Off, Baby" and then, The Last Poets' This Is Madness LP.

Once I focused on music — whether it be avant-garde jazz or cutting-edge rock — I knew I had to be involved with new sounds and sights that were somehow forward-thinking and game-changing.

I loved rock & roll for its expression of aesthetic liberation — and quest for enlightenment. Its passion for life, for a realization that liberation isn't fully possible without a connection to everything around us. That music embraces contradiction and irony. Trying to embrace the entire universe is absurd: you can't be who you are individually while being one with everything else around you.

In science fiction, serious as it can be, there's a celebratory sense of wonder which unleashes a sense of exaltation -- just as great rock does. Music offers contemplative insight without intellectualizing it; you just feel it.

And that is life on the edge. Zigging when I should have zagged and following only the rules that made sense to me. I was always out there, promoting the new and unfamiliar.

As I grew up, I directed my attitude towards ideas which offered new possibilities and supported other kinds of outliers. That's been the driving force of my life — not to dwell on the past, but to transform my interactions with thought leaders and forward thinkers and then pass on what I'd learned to subsequent generations through writing, speaking and other forms of media.

I moved to New York in January 1978, after nearly three years as the Cincinnati Post's rock critic. I knew at the time that I was standing up for something, but I had to do it on a much larger scale than Cincy could bear.

My life's trajectory led to being a pop culture philosopher. It was a way of expressing social criticism while having fun doing it. In the immediacy of the moment, I didn't think I was doing something important, but there I was, memorializing what was occurring at that moment.

The punk "movement" was infused with irony and a hard-edged "don't take oneself too seriously" ethic. But it also possessed morality propelled by a drive to create — like when the Ramones sing "Beat on The Brat" What the fuck was that? It wasn't meant to be taken literally -- it had to be taken ironically with a tongue firmly in cheek. Irony is about layers of meaning, sometimes contradictory, realizing that what's heard or seen is just a layer on the surface -- there's more underneath.

So I became a pop culture chronicler. For half a century, I've documented the worlds of art, film, music, performance and pop culture creators of all sorts. Various actors, directors, artists, musicians, writers, photographers, chefs and entrepreneurs have provided me with many insights. I've offered them in turn to audiences through reviews and interviews. I've been a publisher, editor, columnist, or staffer for many publications — online and in print.

I've spoken with so many from The Rolling Stones and Pearl Jam to writers like William S. Burroughs and Ken Kesey. I spoke with actors the likes of Jennifer Lawrence, Robert DeNiro, Clint

Eastwood, Meryl Streep and many more.

My coverage has attracted millions of readers worldwide in publications ranging from AM-New York, Creem Magazine, Reflex, Heavy Metal. Spin, Vibe, Omni, Look and Seventeen Magazine. In fact, two of my pieces can be read on Spin.com — interviews with The Cure's Robert Smith and George Michael.

With one foot in the analog world and one in the digital space, I took advantage of the internet's advent. Shifting my focus, I began publishing online. I've contributed to HuffingtonPost.com reaching millions of visitors. I've run sites such as Timessquare.com and launched FilmFestivalTraveler.com -- which I published and have been its editor-in-chief.

As the Arts/Features Editor for irishexaminerusa.com, I have a regular platform and regularly contribute to Times Square Chronicles and popentertainment.com. I've hosted a podcast, MUSICARTFILM, and have been a club deejay and magazine publisher. I've produced screening events, panels, workshops and media materials on self-empowerment for musicians, filmmakers and writers.

I created a media consulting company, Insider Media LLC, to advise people on their social media efforts, as well as their online and print start-ups. I have also worked on films doing everything from marketing to script work.

In '79, I discovered the SX-70 Polaroid camera. Out from its compact, sleekly designed frame came a single piece of film which developed before your eyes. But those images had a limited shelf life and would last only if properly stored. Too often, they weren't

During the '80s, I made images of celebs, hip personalities, scenes and even a few nudes. Over time, they got locked away but weren't forgotten. My work has become a goldmine for ideas, stories, articles, exhibitions and books. In digging out those visuals, the past was recalled and illuminated.

Along the way, I've saved everything — media materials, pop culture items, various photos and notes. There's a body of work I created as a writer, editor and consultant while collecting a treasure trove of supportive materials. I've got thousands of magazines, invites, press releases, audio recordings, videos and photos. Plus, there's a vast array of vinyl, CDs and DVDs along with historic collector items like vintage comics, toys and trading cards.

For a long time, this stuff languished in storage — draining resources for no apparent reason. Finally, I decided over 10 years ago to transform this disparate mass of shit from being a hoarders' paradise/nightmare into my "Media Box."

I have hoped it will become a fully realized media institution -- where the many collections (mine and those of others) turn into source material for curated shows, master theses, fashion items, pop culture programming, design inspirations while preserving hundreds of hours of interviews and visual documents.

Wrangling this notion into reality has been an elusive goal with defeats and frustrations. But I'm determined to make the idea so successful that i'll earn a NYTimes obit — or least cause people to wax nostalgic on Facebook.

In creating and opining, I've placed myself within the world of the hip, fashionable, culture-forward and innovative. An advocate for bohemianism, cutting-edge art, progressive visions and alternative lifestyles, I've used the power of "soft culture" to advocate for social change. At times, I've taken an active role — participating in sit-ins and anti-censorship rallies, joining an anti-war march in Washington, holding classes as a guest teacher and being a motivational speaker.

I try to be adept at the latest technologies and have explored activities most would not expect of me — like trying to live off the land during winter. That's made me particular in my choices of friends and lovers — discriminating about where I hang out and who with.

Torn between a struggle for authenticity versus success, money, fame, and power, I've pinioned between one effort and another. That might have kept me from bigger accomplishments, more money and a grander public presence, but I've accomplished enough that there are BB mentions throughout the Wikipedia landscape and online. Google me and you'll see lots of stories along with a few gripes. I'm at the point where I send a bio instead of a resume to get work.

Maybe if I didn't have Midwestern roots, I'd have a more insular NY-native perspective. I'm skeptical about explosive fame and quick burnout. I've avoided some of the emotional and physical pitfalls that others of my generation have succumbed to. But I keep plugging along.

Which brings us to today: Is this enough for a memoir? I hope so.

After writing the above, I stepped back to see what I had. In doing so, I could see what I would share with anyone who wanted to create a memoir of their own.

What of the above would I expand into a book-length memoir? What part requires me to develop the narrative, dialogue or imagery? Where does that leave the discussion for those of you out there considering your own memoir?

How do you get started? Do you create an outline or a chronology?

And that's where I come in. After working directly with so many celebrities -- writing about and with them -- I can improve your first draft or pull the story out from scratch.

The fact is, everyone's life is potentially a story to be documented — whether as a published article or a full-fledged memoir. I'm ready to help you have your own.

*\*\**

To contact Brad:

Cell: 2127299359

bmbmedia53@gmail.com

Social media:

https://www.facebook.com/brad.balfour.9/

https://www.instagram.com/brad.balfour/Twitter

To view writings:

filmfestivaltraveler.com

popentertainmentarchives.com

https://www.huffpost.com/author/brad-balfour

https://www.blackfilm.com/read/?s=Brad+Balfour

https://t2conline.com/?s=brad+balfour

http://irishexaminerusa.com/wp/?s=Brad+Balfour

# Carol M. Moulton

Silence. It's time to finally live a life you feel you belong in. This is why I became a coach. I saw myself in so many women who were struggling but could not clearly identify the source of the problem. That was me. It does not have to be you.

You don't have to be stuck. You don't have to wait a minute longer to change. Make the decision you will no longer participate in a conspiracy of silence to keep you stuck and miserable. The life you want is waiting for you. All you have to do is reach out.

# My Life as a Cautionary Tale

## *by Carol M. Moulton*

The most recent KPMG Women's Leadership Summit Report' found that 75% of executive women feel imposter syndrome throughout their career; and 81% believe they put more pressure on themselves not to fail than men do.

That number is horrific, but not surprising, because I lived it too.

I was anxious to go into business for myself. Hiring my then-husband to work as a business manager, I started my own law firm with no business training, and zero mentorship. All I knew was that I needed to keep good files and make sure I got to court when I was supposed to be there.

Within the first year, I thrived. I made a lot of money and looked good doing it.

But beneath the surface, I was secretly drowning. Money was slipping through the cracks. I had no balance. No fulfillment.

A decade later, I was divorced. Broke. And still questioning if I even deserve to be successful at all.

All I could do was question myself. What happened to me? What happened to my life and the momentum I started with? How did I end up in such a bad relationship? How did I let this man destroy my life's dream?

The truth is, I fell into the same trap many of us do. I was sleepwalking through life, living a story I'd been given, focusing my pain on serving others and often spending money on things that were supposed to fill the hole.

Now you heard those statistics I gave you earlier but let me say it again a different way.

Some of the most powerful women in the workplace are walking around feeling like they don't deserve to be there. The most powerful women in the workplace are pressuring themselves to be perceived as perfect, just to survive. The most powerful women in the workp1ac0 aren't living their best life after making it to the top.

It's a trap. And I was just one of the many women who looked successful but struggled on the inside in ways I couldn't describe.

- Ladies, we've been sold a lie, and this life is killing us.
- We were told to get those degrees, those certifications, those letters behind our names.
- We were told to get that job, the right job, with the right pay.
- We were told to wear the right clothes and do our hair just right. (Translation: For women of color that means "professional" No braids, no locks. I am personally thankful for the CROWN Act — "Create a Respectful and Open World for Natural Hair".)
- We were told to marry this man, have those kids, buy that house. We're told to buy this dress, that bag, this car.
- We're asked to solve everybody's problems but our own.

And all along, there's something bubbling up inside that you can't quite name.

No, you're not crazy. You're just focused on the wrong direction.

I want to help a sister out. Heed what happened next. Change came for me when mentors and friends asked me questions, I couldn't answer. It was through their coaching that I realized how deeply I had internalized my own fear of failure. I was afraid to leave my comfort zone, afraid to make a choice that left me in an unknown place.

I needed to be married, right? People like me are married. I need to do it like this, right? People like me work this way.

I can't talk about these problems, right? People like me are stronger than that.

This is what fear of failure does to us.

It creates perfectionism, which eventually leads to inaction. How can you make decisions if you're fearful of the consequences at every step? How can you make a new choice if you've been told what all the right things are?

That mentorship I received taught me to stop looking past my own experiences and to truly dive deep into who I am, what I really need in my life, and stop ignoring problems. I had to build the skills to be courageous for the first time in my life.

The solution for me was a radical spiritual and intellectual transformation.

What I learned through this moment in my life were these 3 truths.

- Pretending you're fine, doesn't make it so. We can sell others a fantasy but hiding from our problems -- our shame -- doesn't save us from the consequences.

I had a longtime friend, we'll call her Cheryl, who told me that she'd found herself cashing out at the dollar store with an amount equating her monthly rent. She passed it off as a casual comment, but the quiver in her voice told me there was so much more going on. While we may not go as far as spending the rent on discount items, we can find ourselves doing things to relieve the discomfort inside that ends up causing even more problems for us. Whether it's overspending, overeating, or simply sitting actionless (hours on Netflix?) when something needs to change, it all comes from the same place.

- Life issues and work issues will collide. You can't ignore the challenges in your home and think you'll progress at work. It's all part of the same story and each one impacts the other.

My story was a perfect example of this. My husband was part of my business and his poor management of our finances left us penniless and lost me my license. I didn't take care of home, and it had a direct impact on my work life. For others, it may seem less direct, but the impact is still as deep. Your family is struggling, and you feel distracted at work. You're supporting others financially or morally and feeling drained, which impacts your ability to lead. It's all connected, so you can't allow yourself to ignore home and think it will work itself out.

- We cannot grow, and we cannot change, with the same mindset that got us here. **We need a major shift in our consciousness to achieve our personal greatness.**

This almost sounds cliche, but it's also very true. I needed a mentor to help me see myself and my life from a different view. My mind was trained to ignore the truth, to sell a fantasy to myself and others. I was living perfectionism, fear, and refusing to change. You need to renew your mind completely in order to fully shift and become the successful person you want to be.

If you're anything like me, you're probably thinking of all the reasons you don't have the time, the energy, or the money to fix any one of the challenges swirling around in your head right now.

But hear my testimony. The cost of staying in place is far more than the cost of taking action in your life today. For me, staying in place cost me 10 years of my life, a decade of work with no savings to show for it, and years of emotional trauma from the hurt and pain of the betrayal I faced in my marriage.

Once I learned to live courageously, putting aside my pe0ectionism, imposter syndrome and fear, I finally knew where I belonged and how to finally become the woman of strength, I always believed I was.

Dr. Derald Wing Sue is a psychologist and has written several books on the subject of race and race relations in the United States. His books are impactful and cause us to see things we might have no desire to see. Nevertheless, if we are to grow, it is important that we look (and really see) the unvarnished truth.

In one of his books, Race Talk and the Conspiracy of Silence, Dr. Wing Sue discusses the protocols we have silently put in place (and agreed to) of Western culture and that impede authentic dialogue.

I think one of those protocols is particularly important here. Not just in the context of race but in the context of having open and honest conversations with and about yourself.

Dr. Wing Sue defines the Politeness Protocol:

> "We must be nice and polite. We must take care not to offend others. We must keep conversations light, friendly, and noncontroversial. We must avoid conflict. We must embody different selves to maintain social harmony."[1]

How does that feel? Does that fit your life? Is that YOU? Are you rewarded for always being the self-sacrificing, putting others' needs ahead of your own — even when it costs your health, wealth, and sanity? Is that really how we are to live? Is this how you present yourself on the job? Always "nice", "non- controversial", self-sacrificing, anything to get the job done? I am not saying there is anything inherently wrong with any of those things. It is when we are not being our true, authentic selves a problem arises.

Dr. Wing Sue discusses the Politeness Protocol and I believe many of us can find the principles Dr. Wing Sue outlines instructive for our lives. First, there is the Authentic Self — who I really am. What language do you use to express your ideas and beliefs when you are not in fear of being judged?

Can you find yourself here or is it a struggle? It can be if you are ALWAYS concerned about being judged. Judgment is harsh as it leaves no room for grace. And grace is sometimes most difficult to extend to ourselves.

I think of Maya Angelou as demonstrating this quality. Her words were life-giving and touched the soul because of the depth from which her words sprang. And the very young Amanda Gorman has picked up the torch Dr. Angelou left behind.

The next principle is the Ideal Self. This is who you think you are. Now, this one is tricky because you may think of yourself one way but present in an entirely different way. Please take a moment and reflect. How judgmental and critical are you? Is everything around you "wrong?" And if it is to be done correctly, only you can do it? It is very easy to fool yourself, thinking that you are a nice compassionate, giving person when you are actually quite the opposite.

In all honesty, this was me several years ago. I was hyper- critical of everything and everybody. I could spot a flaw from a mile away and did not think twice about sharing this information. Was it helpful? Uplifting? Godly? Not in the least. But I did not SEE it that way. I did not connect my heart to my words and found safety in being critical (perhaps so that no one would look too closely at me.)

I think of many church ladies I have known over the years. They all testify how much they love the Lord but the gossip flows, unending. No shade, just real talk. I love these folk, but I do believe they are, on the whole, some of the most un-self-aware people the good Lord ever put on this planet. And I am saying this with love, not criticism.

For too long, our identity has been rooted in the church, one of the few one places Black folks had a degree of authority. That authority has not always been used well. And all too often, the very people who seek help in the church are embarrassed, thrown away, or just left feeling they want no part of anything called "church." But as my Pastor says, "Eat the meat, throw away the bones." If you are in a place where you are being fed spiritually, separate yourself from the other stuff and get your blessing, child.

Finally, there is the Tactical Self or what I think of as the Instagram Self. That is the Self that is heavily curated to appear perfect. Every meal is perfect. Every drive to the grocery store, perfect. Every aspect of one's life is, check, perfect. There are no babies who throw up or men who cheat. There are no money problems. They think everyone must be jealous because their life is so wonderful. Really? Can that actually be accurate of anyone's life? And how long can that curated life continue?

What happens when the baby gets sick or the man cheats or someone gets fired? What next?

Well, I suggest it is time to stop trying to lead the reality show lifestyle that is void of any semblance to reality. It is really time to stop feeling that fake is better — fake life, fake everything. I knew a woman (this is a true story, I worked with her) — who was very attractive but very insecure. She announced that she was pregnant, but the pregnancy went on for an extraordinarily long time. She was not pregnant; she was wearing a pillow.

She needed to present herself to her husband as with child so he would not leave her. Did it work? Hardly. She ended up in the hospital but not in the maternity ward. My point — you can try to "fake it 'til you make it" but it rarely works. Be the Magnificent You God called you to be. That is so much better than any fake. ("Ain't Nothing Like the Real Thing", said Marvin Gaye and Tammi Terrell).

So - my story? Took me from Catholicism to Islam to the Protestant Church to no church but I found God. I found God in the valley, when I was in the deepest, darkest, place one can imagine. I found that a relationship with Him is better than gold. I also found God has a sense of humor. I once was talking to Him and I complained about getting older. He laughed and said, You're old? Imagine how old I am!" That caught me so off guard, I had to laugh. God is so amazingly wonderful and loving and if you approach Him with your true self, not your curated, self-conscious, inauthentic self, but the real you — the 5-year-old you, the result will be truly amazing. Don't get hung up on the church-y stuff. The dogma and thou-shall-not's. Just breathe and know that He is God. And because He is, you are.

And all I have been through has led me to this moment. The moment where I realize my purpose on earth is to help women who have been through or are going through what I've experienced. The pain, the betrayals, the hurts but like the lotus, able to rise above,

Do you know about the lotus? It grows in mud. But emerges without a trace of it. Let that be you. You have been through some things, but you can some through without a trace of what that looked like. It was an experience, but it is not you.

It's time to be your own advocate. It's time to stop suffering in silence. It's time to finally live a life you feel you belong in. This is why I became a coach. I saw myself in so many women who were struggling but could not clearly identify the source of the problem. That was me. It does not have to be you.

You don't have to be stuck. You don't have to wait a minute longer to change. Make the decision you will no longer participate in a

conspiracy of silence to keep you stuck and miserable. The life you want is waiting for you.

All you have to do is reach out. No pressure. Just pure Sister

love.

To contact Carol:

Website: https://www.MoultonExecutiveCoachino.com LinkedIn: https://www.linkedin.com/in/carol-moulton-481b875/ Facebook: https://www.facebook.com/carol.moulton1

or (240) 207-1872

FOR FURTHER INFORMATION ON CAROL'S COACHING AND PROGRAMS OR JUST TO CHAT, CAROL IS AVAILABLE AT:

---

Advancing the Future of Women in Business: A KPMG Women's Leadership Summit Report, October 2020. Located

at: https://womensIeadership.kpmg.us/summit/kpmy-womens-leadership-report-2020.htm

'i Wing Sue, D. (2015). Race Talk and the Conspiracy of silence: Understanding and Facilitating Difficult Dialogues on Race, Wilev Publishing.

To Contact Carol:

Website: https://www.MoultonExecutiveCoachinq.com LinkedIn: https://www.linkedin.com/in/carol-moulton-481b875/ Facebook:

https://www .facebook.com/carol.moulton1

or (240) 207-1872

# William C. Washington

William C. Washington is "Mind & Music." Becoming a living icon.

William is a Licensed Professional Clinical Counselor, Clinical Hypnotherapist, IFS therapist with Black Therapist Rock, and was a collegiate level adjunct faculty and counseling mentor. He graduated from St. John's Jesuit High School, Xavier University, John Carroll University, and is currently a Ph.D. candidate for the Health Psychology program at Walden University. William has been published as first author, advocating for better health care. He believes we should never choose the better choice, but the HEALTHY one! His passion for your success is felt when he meets you.

William has another side that keeps him grounded. He is a well-accomplished musician, trained in over nine instruments, and has been playing local, national, and international shows. William did his first international tour at 20 years old in Columbia, South America and was on tour with The Temptations. He is currently touring with internationally acclaimed Mourning [A] Blkstar while locally leading Da Land Brass Band based in Cleveland, OH. William has performed and created music in notable areas such as Cartoon Networks Adult Swim, The Kennedy Center, and Christoph Winkler Company in Germany.

During the pandemic, William started a content creating non-profit called "ViewUnity," which has successfully raised over $10,000 with collaborators to help sick kids in hospitals. William stated, "Being myself has been the most challenging and rewarding experience of my life." William is currently looking for his next protége.

# Heal All Ways; Come with Motive, and Leave with Purpose

## By William C. Washington

I grew up believing I could change the world, and I never stopped growing up. Being "William" can have so many meanings, and I found myself in some of the most challenging situations because I never understood the power of my own story. To be a Washington man in my family was to live by a standard that worked twice as hard to get half of what "they" had. As a child, I wanted to be a taxicab driver because I could always go somewhere and meet new people (before Uber was even an idea). I also thought that being a dentist would change my whole life, and my family would finally be proud of me. My brother and I (who eventually became a fantastic physician) would own a clinic together, and I would finally earn my place in the world. My family believed in the American dream, and honestly, I still do… But the sequel.

I was denied from dental schools, and it took every dream I held so dearly away. The feeling of rejection is one thing… but putting in the work, staying up late, studying all week wasn't enough. Rejection creates a brief moment where you start to question the worth of your ability and impact. The feeling of denial can sit inside you for weeks, even years, and changes how you look at needing help. I started living in a state of survival and lived in impulsive cycling, not recognizing my worth. Surviving in failure feels like window shopping, and everyone else is somehow affording everything you can't. I had to find the price of acceptance to feel like I could start again. I found that the cost of acceptance is yourself. No one else can pay for who you will become, and knowing your self-worth is living your experience to the fullest.

I sat for months trying to open doors that were not mine, and I had to learn acceptance. I went back to school to make myself more competitive for dental schools and was a janitor and musician to make money. I found my nights cleaning the facilities as one of the most peaceful times because I was a part of progress, and it let me think about the cards dealt in my life. Within the first month of being a janitor, I got employee of the month. I was so proud of that because

I give everything, I have in any situation to make sure I am myself. I accepted the certificate with such joy after going through such rejection. Two days later, I received a call asking if I wanted to play for the Temptations and I would have to move to Tennessee. I was on tour for a year and saw another lifestyle I never thought was possible. I realize you are only as open to experiences as much as you are hurt from. Being on tour and learning the stories of other artists made me think about my own story and who I truly am. I decided to go back to school, but not for dentistry. I learned that listening was a skill that everyone needed.

You see, I am a therapist by day, musician by night. Being a worldwide healer required audacity to own the story only I could tell. The more you tell your story, the less you become of it. The uncanny thing is I found my most authentic moments in my losses and hardships. Humility kept me alive. I created the Washington Wellness Institute to provide a healing center for those just as lost as I was. I was frustrated, burned out, suicidal, and unsure of how to make an impact in my life. But I had an energy that would never go away, and there was something that kept pushing me to have this attitude of wanting more.

Have you ever eaten an entire plate of food and knew you could go back in line but didn't want people to notice? When you live your purpose, you forget people are watching. I tried so hard in my life to be seen, but when I found my purpose, I only wanted to make sure I was who I needed to be for the bigger picture. You'll find that unhappy people can smell a happy person a mile away, but never taste it. After years of research in psychology and performing tours on national stages, I found one thing in common: Everyone is trying to be themselves but doesn't know if they should. It was at that moment I realized that I needed to make something that may not change the world but give someone the chance to change their world.

I created Restorative Enhancement Management, REM, to help the individual find their purpose and create internal reciprocity through a 5-step principle philosophy to address their distress. I found limitations as a therapist and wanted to go beyond sitting in a chair for 60 mins. I found limitations as an artist and wanted to be able to live in harmony regardless of how unsure life presented itself. Even when you do the things you love, there's always more of yourself to give. REM gave me a level of peace in my purpose and let me process and heal at the same time. I couldn't believe the philosophy I made gave my clients a sense of purpose beyond my own training.

The first principle is, "The action is never the reason." I found many people who were trying to find their purpose living by motive, creating instant gratification or self-sabotage. The second principle is, "Unmet needs result in irrational behaviors." Whenever you lose who you are on the inside, you seek false things on the outside. The third principle, "Time is a resource used for limitation or application." We always feel limited when we don't understand what is truly ours to use. Invest in your autonomy and find opportunities around the corner. The fourth principle is, "Be everything, expect nothing." Understanding who you are in the spaces you show up in are accents to who you want to be. I choose competence over confidence in my experiences, and it creates healthier boundaries when owning your story. The fifth principle is, "Purpose is the human compass." When you feel unsure about why you exist, the first question is asking yourself, "What do you want to be known for?" When you finally come to your purpose, the weight of people, places and things won't hold you back as they once did. With self-awareness comes emotional responsibility.

I would use REM with clients and found them seeing their mental health and trauma decrease. It was amazing seeing their ability to become emotionally responsible actively changing. In REM you process uphill and heal downhill, giving the individual the ability to applicate their growth. Going uphill is to help gain the perspective needed to see all the obstacles in your way, but going downhill is just as careful because you have to pace the peace you learn to accept. Acknowledging the difference to make the difference separates the good from the great.

We believe, in REM, there are four emotional cancers. These emotional cancers grow within you and cause you to live by motives, which remove you from your purpose. The four emotional cancers are the following: reactions, rationalizing, regret, and resentment. There are things in your life that have gone unresolved or unanswered and unfortunately, they still live in how we interact day to day. When you react and not respond, you mentally lose your integrity, feeling emotionally compromised. Think about all the times you had challenging moments and thought of the perfect response after the fact. When you begin rationalizing the importance of how you feel, you let others decide how much you matter moving forward. That moment can create regret if you don't address the issues that caused you stress. Resentment is knowing what the problem is, but you feel helpless, and unwanted behaviors or feelings occur. This creates negative projections or deflections. REM helped me navigate processing and restoring the motive-based feelings.

I couldn't believe that every moment I experienced in life fell under a principle of REM, and what was even better was that I felt in control of myself, even when I was lost. I saw REM changing people in ways I never saw in standard therapeutic work. They could take REM with them, live through it, and make it something special on their own. I teach that therapy happens in the session, and healing happens in the application. REM became the answer.

I can't think of having a bad day anymore because, with options, there are results I can choose from. Motives have become red flags when discovering the truth in intention for me and others. The hardest thing right now to accept in today's society is living in a world you don't choose yourself in. These principles gave me five reasons to think bigger, be bigger, and live bigger. I found my stress had a story, and there was nurturing that was needed. I knew I was the main character of my story, but I needed to be a better writer, and REM gave me the preparation to get back to that. I stand today healing the world of others, fulfilling my dream to be a cycle breaker.

I never thought that Restorative Enhancement Management would become the foundation of my dream and the answer to so many other people. I simply knew that I wanted to wake up knowing I had a way of life that celebrated who I am. Purpose is a beautiful thing because it has no direction, it is a way of life, and you are invited to hold onto your own. You are the compass in your journey if you believe in what you do. Internal reciprocity is knowing you're worth and spending everything you got. You still feel enough after every moment because it is meaningful. So back to dinner, Are you ready for the next plate?

***

To contact William:

If you want to contact, become part of the REM journey, or want guidance, please contact me at info@wwillc.org. Look at our website, www.washingtonwellnessinstitute.org, and follow on Facebook or IG (@Wash_Wellness). We are also on Youtube as Washington Wellness Institute.

# Diane A. Curran

Steeped in the creative arts from her earliest memories, Diane A. Curran, The Wow Whisperer, is passionate about the role and value of high-performance communications in life, business marketing, and the classic fine arts, especially painting, design and modern media. She is a branding expert and marketing consultant and who makes marketing creative for audiences via messaging, design, and interactive strategies.

Some people consider speaking in public a fate worse than almost anything. Diane's gigs include 4600+ public speaking presentations, art tours led, media performances, teaching, training, and leading events of many types and audience sizes. Add 3000+ networking events in her career, and she has a wealth of secrets and stories she's always delighted to share.

With marketing & creative projects done for thousands of professionals shaping her vision, she knows the pulse of the good, the ugly and the extraordinary that impacts communications success. A fountain of creativity, Diane knows what's missing in most presentations is ease, play and connection.

Diane's signature podcast is "Wow Whispering" for which she is developing her third series for airing. You can find it on Podopolo, Apple Podcasts, Stitcher, Amazon, Podbean, and Google, where she and her guests from many walks of life explore wows and whispers in the Heart of Conversation, and exchange original ideas in warm, engaging episodes.

# How Do You Know When You're Been Wowed?

## *By Diane A. Curran*

Truth be told, wow itself is a quirky word. Most people can't give you a definition for it at all. And I've asked!

There's barely a worthwhile definition in any dictionary that I've opened, none to pinpoint its real energy. Yet the word wow has been traced back to the Scots in history, with its first recorded appearance in the early 16th century.

Yet people certainly do know when they're in the midst of feeling wowed.

When the word "Wow!" is voiced, you, or maybe someone near you, is having a moment. You can tell by how people slip into a faraway dreamy look when you ask them to remember a wow they've felt or seen.

### How Business Can Wow

I became fascinated with the word wow itself in my own business a couple of decades in… ever since I started noticing that clients would often say just one word when I unveiled creative branding and logo graphics or shared a new communications concept for their growth.

"Wow!" they'd say.

That single, unprompted, indefinable word. It held everything from emotional excitement to visions of possibility, and quickening questions about what to do next. All in a word with just three little letters and no universal definition.

I heard "Wow!" enough that I took it on for my own business branding. People naturally smiled about "The Art and Science of Your Wow! Factor" when I said it. When heading to the podium or microphone in networking groups, people would just shout "Wow!" and we'd grin at each other, as I said nothing… and smiled a split second longer than you might expect. My audience knew there was a swift riddle or story snippet coming, and they were up for being surprised by me with something they couldn't predict I'd say.

Wow wasn't about shocking my audience, and definitely not about hard sell or shouting them into submission. It was always about opening us up to be together— to enter the unknown, where we could "Wow!" together.

Your audience is always the smartest brain trust in the room, real or virtual. They give the courtesy of their time while holding their smarts close to the vest as they size you up, skeptical faces politely veiled.

Any audience always wants more of the real wows. Like the puppy that races to retrieve the ball, then bounds toward you so excited for you throw it again that sometimes they forget to drop the ball first. Maybe they want a little fun chase. Then again and again they run back to you, until you're both out of breath, you laughing, their tongue waggling, happy to sit, pant and relax together.

It's tempting to consider money as the ultimate measure for wow in business. We live in an era when not only businesses, but institutions of all kinds try to define themselves with money and metrics. They are measurable, with a surface aura of objectivity, commandeering the mic, demanding attention as they compete to win biggest-as-best.

**I propose something more magnetic as evidence that wow is in the air.**

Wow brings you and others together.

Whether it's you and your clients, you and your team, you and your larger community, there is an exchange of value more far-reaching than money or winning against others in the metrics trap.

Wow joins you and others together in shared experiences of inspiration, transformation, and even trust. It's naturally magnetic.

Notice when you and those you seek to connect with have done so, because wow is in the mix, and trust and loyalty are about to arise authentically,

### How Dreams Can Wow

Dreams can wow if you give them enough room to reveal their messages.

## Dream One: Runway Nightmare

Some of you may know of a TV reality series about fashion runways that's been on air for at least 18 years. I'm a devoted fan, and pore over the details of every episode with a close friend every time it's on.

Well, one day, my dreamtime self-decided it was time to make my leap into fashion design at warp speed. Or more accurately, wrap speed! I call it My Fashion Runway Early Morning Nightmare.

We join this dream already in progress, as often happens to me...

Three other remaining competitors plus myself were left in the semi-finals. We were given a surprise assignment to work inside a floaty funky weird, overstuffed boutique.

Our clients were ladies who were very pretty, but they had never been professional models. They would choose their own fabric and go buy it, but not at the legendary fabric store used in most episodes. Uh oh!

We were supposed to design and sew three "looks" each, compressed into a single 4- or 5-hour stretch of time.

My lady was very late arriving, then went to go in search of fabric for her task but came back with no fabric at all after a long time.

Now I had only 15 minutes to come up with all three looks, plus no workspace, no sewing machine, no table, and no fabric. So, I pulled scarves from the boutique's retail displays to pin together a dress.

My model expected she would now go get hair & makeup done. I decided," No makeup, no hair. Stay right here!!" and the show's producer & another designer supported me.

I started the first look with four scarves I'd found with shoes and jewelry from inside the boutique. I pinned one scarf into a wrap with faux dolman sleeves. The other three scarves made up the draped-pinned dress itself. I had more scarves for other looks, but absolutely no time to make them, eek. But at least my model was not naked for the runway!

Suddenly, I woke at dawn, despite trying to actually stay asleep and use last the 15 minutes before the runway show, hoping I could dream them all into existence on time.

Alas, no more time to finish, either the fashion looks or the dream…

So I got up in real life, and bee-lined to my computer. Scribbling a few words to document this vision would not suffice, so I launched my graphics software and drew that fashion ensemble at break-neck speed while I could remember it, visualizing what I had created as the dream's look #1. Nightmare over ;-) Whew.

I posted the illustration and dream summary on one of my social media pages right away. I never did get to finish the dream and find out if I won against all odds. Exhausted, I was wowed by somehow bridging the gap from dreamtime designing to real world art illustration.

*Dream Two: Dream Home*

In the midst of a 1990s long-distance romance (me in CA, he in AZ) I had an unusually vivid dream one night. Mostly, I forget my dreams, because as you can read in the one above, they can be exhausting!

Anyway, I was living in The Valley in LA, in an architecturally boring 1BR cookie-cutter 70's era apartment building at that time.

The dream floats into my sleep time… and I realize I'm being shown a new apartment that looks suspiciously like a cottage of the tiny kind.

It has dark interior wood paneling, but it looks nicely handcrafted. It seems to have vertical casement windows in its one-room corners, and some sort of built-ins everywhere to store books, canned goods, decorations, clothing, you name it. It reminds me of the super spare little cottages that dotted Cape Cod in Massachusetts where I'd stayed overnight with my dad and brother twice as a treat while a kid. Because they were summer cottages, they were not insulated, and they used the support beams and bracing slats as storage shelf cubbyholes.

As I was looking at this and marveling at this cottage's little nooks, my current romantic partner floated into the dream (… people never seem to walk in my dreams; they float with the greatest of ease) and I telepathically asked him how he liked it.

Naturally, I woke up without his answer, or what this little cottage/studio was all about, so I called him on the phone in real life to ask what he thought it meant. His answer was simply "I don't know." Alrighty then!

Well, not long after, the pre-dawn Northridge Earthquake bounced me out of bed in my boring apartment (I was too close for comfort to the epicenter, so bouncing was indeed the operative word) almost 24 hours to the minute the day after my mother had died on the East coast.

Suddenly in the aftermath, while shivering through repeated aftershocks as I thought about my Mum's eternal adventure just beginning, I was in the market for a new place to live. At a random rental-finder service popular at the time, I found an attached guest house, surrounded by a garden my mother would have loved, and was selected from many applicants to move in.

Yes, it was really quite tiny, but thankfully only one story, no one above or below me, and my jangled nerves felt safer by the hour. A few days after moving in, with it barely furnished, I was sitting in an armchair in the middle of this tiny studio when my eyes finally opened to the the details of my surroundings.

This very studio, with its handcrafted paneling, corner casement windows, and cleverly inset built-in cabinets and closets abounding, was the cottage from my dream! Wow was the only word that would do.

**Dreams have no interest in something most of us allow to run (ruin?) our lives.**

Time. And especially the clocks we invented to measure time.

The two dreams I shared here treated time completely differently as I reconsider them.

The Dream Home had no clock, and no mention of time at all. If anything, it assumed an aura of being in the present, which I was unable to place in any context that I could act upon when I awoke.

The Runway Nightmare was utterly time-obsessed, with 15-minute deadlines stoking impending doom for me at every moment in the contest at hand. None of the tasks went according to plan!

Yet both dreams wowed me in their own way. Together they wove a bigger story, years apart, and only now is it dawning on me consciously.

With the Dream Home, I was wowed in mere weeks of real life. I was bounced into a completely new home, and had no clue from the dream, or any interpretation I sought out, that this was about to happen, and quickly. Earthquakes have a way of reminding us how much the unknown runs the show!

For the Runway Nightmare, I felt compelled by its energy to race in real life to use my computer and draw the dream's dress design. I suppose it's not that different than doing fast-paced design work for clients when inspiration comes to me from the ethers or waking dreams.

I felt I was failing in that Runway Nightmare, as it tore away from me before I could finish my task. Little did I know that the invisible cosmic clock was counting down that frantic 15 minutes for five long years until a worldwide pandemic truncated not just my plans, but everyone's tasks, timetables, health, and many precious goals and dreams. I'd never expected such a glacially slow reveal to a wow.

The Wow of Dreams requires us to stay present while being grounded in both patience and action.

Patience and action are not born enemies, no matter how often we humans set them against each other. An elusive secret is that we can make them allies within ourselves. Slow and fast each have a contribution to make. For me, slowing down enough to feel grounded corrects my habit of racing so fast in daily life that I run out of time, oddly enough. The pandemic gave me plenty of time to practice all that as even non-Covid health challenges demanded that I slow way down. Wow!

The Wow of Dreams has an added bonus to offer once you start embracing patience and action as allies. That's when it begins to drop hints about the power of Not Knowing. Shhh! Lest our noisy curiosity chase Not Knowing back into unfathomable shadows. I'll be quiet about this for now and move on.

## Is It Time to Offer a Definition of Wow?

We may have started wandering through our own memories of wow as these dream vignettes unfolded here.

A few years ago, I created what follows as a definition, and it continues to open up my perspective on what wow is. Diane's definition…

> **Wow: An Intuitive, instinctive expression voiced in awe, pleasure, or stun when presented with the unexpected.**

We've touched on several of the more appealing aspects of wow, but one we have not yet explored jumps out in this definition.

## The Challenges of Stun

Consider that we know we're inside a "Wow" when we say it out loud spontaneously, often unaware we're about to say it. It's stimulated by moments of awe, or pleasure, or even the "stunning" excitement of beauty, joy, or a delightful surprise.

We even use the word stunning as shorthand for beautiful, dazzling, breathtakingly attractive.

But we know that the word stun can signal experience of a very different kind.

As I write these words, we've navigated the often stunning and tragic difficulties of a worldwide pandemic. It has taught us the hard way that the unexpected is woven into the very essence of life.

Definitions attempt to evoke nuances that words seek to explain objectively. Words are meant to be useful in clarifying meaning.

When we learn a new language, we go at it much faster than babies do, usually thinking and memorizing rather than simply immersing ourselves in a lived experience. We are often frustrated by what are called idiomatic expressions that convey the energy behind an often-illogical combination of words that native speakers grasp deeply in their psyches.

The energy behind words is what we hint at when we say we have a meeting of the minds with someone, or we refer to a special someone as a soulmate or kindred spirit. We want to go beyond words to enjoy common understanding, common connection and common ground.

Words seek to evoke the energy of wow.

However, in a world still grappling with health mysteries not yet tamed, environmental factors far from resolved, inequities and much more, we humans are also an example of the destructive reality of what stun can mean.

Stun can surface amidst overwhelm, conflict, violence, war, and fear.

Fear is considered a primal emotion, and our reactions to it are often instinctive, which speaks to a core aspect of wow.

We've seen others, maybe even found ourselves, caught short of breath at some awful moment, saying "Wow!" as an expression of revulsion. It strikes unexpectedly.

Stun often means being shocked into a temporary inability to react, or worse, to being knocked or dazed into an unconscious state. We're frozen spectators, unable to look away or resolve what stuns us in those moments.

**How Life Can Wow**

My suggested definition of wow intentionally combines the the intuitive and instinctive. This is intended to provide a new option to remind us that we humans have the power to forge new neural pathways, even under duress, that do not dead-end in permanent entrapment, or the subjugation that destructive stunning is meant to impose.

We can instead ally the power of intuition and instinct. In recognizing that they are often treated as opposites in their emotional root and physical expression, we can learn that they are not opposites.

Just as I suggested that patience and action are not born enemies, and that we can make them allies within ourselves, so it is with intuition and instinct.

When intuition and instinct align, then further ally with patience and action, no amount of destructive intention can outlast what they make possible. Because what they make possible opens up many new healing pathways.

And when fear learns that Not Knowing is not its enemy, fear can discover that war in all its horror is not the final arbiter or ruler it claims to be.

## Have You Been Wowed Lately?

To help us answer this question, I'd like to pair the word wow with another of my favorite words… whispering. Naturally I have a definition to offer for that word, too. Diane's definition…

> **Whispering: Using a soft, confidential tone or manner to hint at or deliver a private message.**

Each of these words seemed to possess very different energy signatures.

> Wow is Spontaneous. Open. Expressive.
> Whispering is Intimate. Still. Receptive.

People's self-expression often seems to gravitate more toward one or the other, though in reality we are a unique and variable blend of both.

In fact we need to ponder both wows and whispers when we consider what messages, impulses, and inspirations have caught our attention lately.

How receptive are you to wise whispers, or exuberant wows, or both? They help you focus on what's now or next for you, bringing you present to inner guidance, the light of spirit, or a higher power of inspiration.

You may hold certain whispers deep in your heart, quietly nurturing them as a source of nourishment, rest, and respite for your own peace of mind.

You may relish more public excitement, risks, or adventures, freely sharing your gung-ho energy as you live life like there's every tomorrow.

Life is overflowing with the unexpected, a capable partner to the unknown. "Not Knowing" frees you to notice the wows and whispers arising in your life's ebb and flow.

Your unique, ever-fluid journey is your gift to all of us, and we thank you in advance for the discoveries you'll make and share with us.

Let people wow you, one at a time or collectively, just as you're already wowing us!

***

To contact Diane:

www.TheMarketingDeal.com

www.WowWhispering.com

https://www.facebook.com/WowWhispering

https://www.facebook.com/TheMarketingDeal

https://twitter.com/wowdianeacurran

https://www.linkedin.com/in/dianeacurran/

https://www.instagram.com/themarketingdeal/

https://themarketingdeal.com/amazonTMD

# Dr. Jackie Lau

Dr. Jackie Lau is a neuroscientist and an award-winning international life coach, who is fascinated with human behaviors and the mechanisms underlying our mental and emotional states. With a deep appreciation for the integrative approach of modern psychology, neuroscience and spirituality, Jackie is a top life coach in Australia and has co-created with people all over the world to radically transform into more self-awareness, sense of purpose and inner freedom.

Jackie is trained as a strategic interventionist and breakthrough specialist, which combines effective techniques evolved from neurolinguistic, psychological, and therapeutic inter-disciplines. As a curious researcher, Jackie completed her Ph.D. in neuroscience at the Garvan Institute of Medical Research, Sydney Australia, studying the neural circuits governing motivation and reward. She is currently researching on neurodegenerative diseases in Hong Kong, investigating the molecular basis relating neuroplasticity to cognition.

Leveraging her diverse cultural background, Jackie is profoundly devoted to studying Eastern and Western philosophy and literatures, learning transformative wisdom from influential spiritual teachers. She loves the art of music and dance. Jackie is trained as a classical violinist from a young age, later on discovered her passion in classical guitar, and has also been a dedicated hip-hop dancer and instructor since her college years.

Jackie's vision is to empower the human family to tune in consciously and align with our authentic virtuous Self, to live passionately and creatively with full presence.

# From self-love to Self-love

## By Dr. Jackie Lau

### I.  Coincidence or guidance?

Our experience of life can be complicated until it can be not. It can be one with millions of decisions leading to another decision at any point in time, or one with millions of decisions leading to the letting go of resistance to guided intuitions.

*Get curious with the gift of your sense of resistance, it offers more wisdom and cosmic comfort than all perceived conveniences combined.*

It was 4:00 in the morning. I was still sitting at McDonald's hogging a quiet spot next to a plug socket, determined to aimlessly watch stand-up comedy specials on my laptop till my next flight in three hours.

After all it was finally the Christmas season, I could not be more ready to take a break and see my folks after a week-long conference in Germany and plentiful sleep deprivation halfway through grad school.

> "The breeze at dawn has secrets to tell you.
> Don't go back to sleep.
> You must ask for what you really want.
> Don't go back to sleep.
> People are going back and forth across the doorsill where the two worlds touch.
> The door is round and open.
> Don't go back to sleep."
> — Rumi

Just as I was simultaneously dozing off and vigilantly noticing how freakishly quiet the familiar Kuala Lumpur International Airport was, considering it was the festive season.

"Excuse me?" A woman in her 50s with black frame glasses asked politely. "Where can I find an adaptor for charging my phone?" Her accent gave her away that she's a fellow Aussie.

"Don't think you can find anything in the wee hours. Happy to be your savior with the collection of charging cables I've got." I put on a cheeky smile, gesturing for her to sit next to me - at this point I would enjoy any company.

We spent the next three hours sharing wonders.

With her beautiful child-like spirit and kind eyes, I wasn't surprised yet felt incredibly delighted to learn that she was the founder at Wellspring Initiative Cambodia – an organization founded in 2013, working on the streets with the "invisible" community of homeless children and their families, some were found begging at the traffic lights, to bring God's love and transformation in Phnom Penh Cambodia.

It was a seemingly simple encounter that spoke to and touched my heart on many levels, particularly at a stage of my felt existential and identity crisis. Despite having the fortune to have never experienced any of the four mental breakdowns on average per doctorate degree that others speak of, I was inevitably going through waves of overwhelm as a young neuroscientist – the futility of the academic publishing machine, the unforeseeable translatability of medical research to meaningful health practices, the incessant search for fulfilment through an external identity and a functional role.

"May I offer you a prayer?" She placed her hand on my forehead with a beatific smile, interrupting my deep thoughts with an inexplicable sense of knowingness that "This has to be the long-waited profound experience that opens me to myself."

"I can see the shadow of you on a mountaintop, in front of a herd of sheep..." She opened her eyes and realized it was time to run for her connecting flight to Melbourne.

I was left spellbound and deeply humbled, with an intense realization of the unmistakable and auspicious sign of a powerful shift within me, one that is revealed many years later to serve as a beacon for my journey to alignment, expansion and service.

## II. Self-love: inheritance or birthright?

With a deep appreciation for the combinative approach of neurolinguistic, psychological, and spiritual inter-disciplines, I have co-created with people all over the world in the last decade to transform into more self-awareness, sense of purpose and inner freedom. Along the path of transcendence into self-realization, one theme that we always wind up with no matter the challenge, from trauma to relationships to business building, is "self-love".

> *"Love is a state of Being. Your love is not outside; it is deep within you. You can never lose it, and it cannot leave you. It is not dependent on some other body, some external form."* — Eckhart Tolle

We are often told that love, or love for oneself, is an intrinsic capacity, both innate and inherited; it does not depend on any external circumstances or personal traits. Why, then, do we feel that "self-love" is so hard to attain? We are not looking for rainbow and unicorn, but a default felt sense of joy and contentment. Why the cross-cultural, cross-gender, cross-age struggle?

What if we have got it the other way round all long? Rather than "effort-ing": to figure out how to attain "self-love", and to seek something that is perceived as outside of ourselves…what if we start "love-ing": to first understand how we have blocked ourselves from recognizing this natural state, and to relax the patterns that hinder connection to our true nature?

> *To tune in and truly see the blocks we have built around our own love opens the gateway to grace and flow.*

## III. "Self"-love does not rely on "otherness"

*"Respect was invented to cover the empty place where love should be."* — Leo Tolstoy

*So much about the theme of "self-love" is conceptualized around a sense of separation with others today.*

It may be fair to say that people cross paths in the "self-love" ideation often have had our fair bit of sufferings due to external circumstances and our ongoing relationships to them. Let's take things simply, humbly and lovingly.

There is much and increasing attention given in our society to the invention and use of terminology that emboldens the illusion that we are separate – narcissists, sociopaths, malignant people, energy vampires, etc. And then there are the ones that gained instant creditability and armor through coating with seemingly righteous and positive connotations, such as healthy boundaries, spiritual boundaries, private life, personal matter.

It is tempting, especially when we feel pain, to conclude situations or people with a simple label, with a self-diagnosis or a self-directed diagnosis of others, without attempting to understand the source and cause of such perception.

*"There are no facts, only interpretations."* — Friedrich Nietzsche

*Question is, how much of our interpretations is actually the reflection of our own projections or shadow?*

All forms of generalization are created to soothe our hurt expectations from specific events or people, to move our attention from a curious and intimate place to one of complacency, apathy and resistance to understand the "general groups".

"He wouldn't answer my calls, exactly like what they say about them narcissists!"

"Asian parents are all like this, why bother telling them my dream of becoming a comedian. I'm not ready to be a doctor or a lawyer anytime soon…"

"I should stop hanging out with them vegan paleo keto fanatics, they are always on my back about every food item I barely glanced at."

*We invent internal dialogues to externalize how we truly feel; all forms of perceived rejection operate ultimately through our sense of powerlessness against another.*

Imagine a state of being, where a deep sense of peace and wellbeing does not rely on our guardedness from others whom we perceive, from their temporary expressions, as "weak" or "negative" or "toxic" - fleeting traits that we sometimes also unconsciously exhibit.

### IV. Mirror, mirror on the wall, who is the barest of them all?

> *"Projection is one of the commonest psychic phenomena... Everything that is unconscious in ourselves we discover in our neighbour, and we treat him accordingly.... Not that these others are wholly without blame, for even the worst projection is at least hung on a hook, perhaps a very small one, but still a hook offered by the other person."* — Carl Jung

What we see in others often serves as a reflection of our relationship with ourselves - the way we connect with others starts with connectedness within.

Let's suspend any resistance and skepticism for a moment, and be open to the idea that, given the same life experiences, past conditioning, core values, level of consciousness, we would all do exactly the same as another.

To be more specific, what if our tendency to externalize our source of discomfort is the cause AND result of emotions that have been repressed, suppressed and avoided? And the resistance to look within is putting us at a default state of heightened involuntary reactivity? Hence more vulnerable to the temptations of separateness and further externalization?

We therefore see the world through the lens of our unresolved emotions and are ready to identify anything as triggers for us to react to, as means to release some of the constant tension that we feel. This projection mechanism is often manifested as externalization of the disconnection we feel with ourselves on the inside – subconsciously or unconsciously, we set heavy boundaries with others in order to normalize a sense of disintegration with ourselves.

> *"When you squeeze an orange, you'll always get orange juice to come out. It doesn't matter who does the squeezing. What comes out is what's inside."* — Wayne Dyer

Here is an example of a common pattern we go into for nursing our sense of otherness: in order to avoid confronting our inner issues, we create mental scenarios where we conclude another's identity through selectively labeling their momentary expressions, to which we felt victimized. We then get fixated on our version of the story through perpetually casting ourselves the victim and avoidance of confrontation with another, for consideration and understanding of another's perspectives in a real conversation may threaten the sense of significance we get from blaming. In time, to stay in the "at effect" position and escape from external and internal confrontation, we go into false acceptance and generalize this projection as the nature of the world.

We have all heard "It is what it is. I have tried and some people are just like this. I pick my battles…with some people, you just have no control."

What if, as law of attraction puts simply, because we reject and avoid ourselves, we perceive others as rejecting and avoiding us. We are then triggered to reject and avoid others first before feeling our own rejection and avoidance. It is almost like a "self"-regulating feedback loop.

Eventually, the progressive externalization of our feelings and experiences becomes some type of social conditioning in our society — we all live in a big bubble of choppy connections derived from self-denial packaged as political correctness, comprising smaller isolated bubbles of individuals tiptoeing around shinny mirrors of self-reflection.

### V. The little s and the big S. Does size really matter?

*"Whenever two people meet, there are really six people present. There is each man as he sees himself, each man as the other person sees him, and each man as he really is."* — William James

What if I propose to you that self-love can be realized and actualized simply through the process of recognizing the "Self"?

Our disintegrated selves feed on the disintegration between the little self and the big Self. As much as we know that words and labels don't really represent the true essence of anything other than the trap of the intellect, yet since the language we use shapes our model of the world, and the concepts about ourselves and others, let's willingly get stuck on the level of words for a moment.

Most of who we think we are derives from the little self – ego identity, the survivor, dualistic, "self"-seeking through sense of separation from others, fear-based judgements and "at effect" victimhood.

And then there is the big Self, the undefined and unmanifested, the "at cause" creator, non-dualistic, one-with-all consciousness.

> *"The Tao that can be told is not the eternal Tao; The name that can be named is not the eternal name. The nameless is the beginning of heaven and earth."* — Laozi

Much like "Oh this must be a moment of no-thought that the masters speak of!" during meditation, which is itself a thought, identification with the big Self is just another attempt to feed the ego identity, or specifically the spiritual ego, through spiritual materialism.

The Self is inconceivable yet impeccable, and is often retrospectively realized through our inner awareness, from then on it cannot be un-realized or un-known.

> *"No matter what the practice or teaching, ego loves to wait in ambush to appropriate spirituality for its own survival and gain."* — Chögyam Trungpa

Imagine a forgetful frog that wakes up every day with amnesia. One day, having spent most of the afternoon on a marshland, he decides to explore the neighborhood and stumbles across a lake. Seeing water for the first time, curiosity gets the best of him. He dips one leg to test the depth of the water. To his surprise, he instantly feels revitalized by the moisture soaked through his skin into his body. Only then did he realize how dried out his skin has been. He can no longer deny his natural inclination to return to his home of water — suddenly he remembers, that is where he started off as a tadpole.

This is basically how we live – letting the little self run the show until our skin dries out and we can no longer deny the big Self.

> *"You say, I'll make believe you are who you think you are if you make believe I am who I think I am."* — Ram Dass

Most of us are conditioned and socialized to compulsively conceptualize who we are through what we have, what we know, and what we do. We categorize our and others' actions and behaviors, as soon as they come into our awareness, as some polarized things with a degree of intrinsic goodness or badness, to constantly feed our egoic mind's need for dualism. Our sensitivity to life is compromised when we live in this predicament – we miss the essence of our vision outside our predetermined knee-jerk reactions to situations; we miss the beauty of Beings, independent of their relationship and function to solely our "selves".

> *"The moment people remember that they've forgotten is a moment of grace."* — Barbara De Angelis

The journey of Self-transformation has begun with our willingness to see the misalignment and alignment within our "selves", and between ourselves and others, to come to realize the nature of reality.

Instead of falling into the habitual entrapment of dualistic judgement and resistance, we can allow more. Gently tune into a sense of curiosity and acceptance, to give more rather than to demand for more, to see a more harmonic world.

*Our curiosity about ourselves and others is directly proportional to our degree of openness to express our authentic Self.*

### VI. Expanding awareness to the impersonal oneness
*When I stop believing in opposites, I see myself in all.*

Have you ever wondered that everything we say, know and do is picked up from someone and somewhere else, in order to socialize and be socialized, to condition and re-condition, to learn and unlearn? There is no such actual thing as "my" rituals, "my" ways, "my" life. We all exist in relation and connection to the ever evolving everything else.

There come the questions, "Must I fear what others fear?" "Are my fears even mine?" "If not, where did I pick them up and when do I put them down?"

Consider that – change is natural. There is actually immense energy going into staying the same in stagnation, into resisting the natural waves of change and the rhythm of nature.

*Perhaps, 'I invented nothing' is a helpful reminder for an ongoing return to flexibility and sensitivity to life.*

Since all human experience comes from within, what if we can turn our strength and effort for self-protection and survival reinforcement into power for Self-awareness and unity?

> *"First there is a mountain, then there is no mountain, then there is."* — Donovan Leitch, inspired by Qingyuan Weixin

Unity and oneness is not defined or potentiated by a lack of diversity, or fear of differences, it is an innate place of raw peace and creation that we spontaneously return to, where ego dances, openness and love shines — all part of the divine play.

*Through profound introspection on the paths to inner freedom, one can realize the kind of transcendent connection with the infinite oneness that is within all of us, through which we can connect with each other in a different way, collectively we can have a different kind of power.*

"With great power comes great responsibility." — François-Marie Arouet (or Uncle Ben in Spider-Man)

### VII. Healing from self-love to Self-love

*Self-love does not depend on the others, nor the seeming otherness of the seeming others.*

Much attention has been placed on the theme of "healing" in the self-"help" communities. Is it actually helpful to focus on "healing"?

There is every day healing from mental and emotional loads, to cleanse our mind and body from external and internal stimuli and thought forms and reactionary cravings. It is wonderful to bring awareness to "unloading".

On the other side, there is to heal "from an experience" or "from the past", presupposing there is a place of significance in the past, where originated the gap between the "less-than-whole" and the "whole" Self.

*In this sense, the concept of healing is affixed to the idea of the past combined with the identification with an "at effect" mental position with past events.*

To "heal" then presupposes us to first come from a place of "lack", and through the process of healing, return to wholeness — some form of destination or endpoint to get to eventually.

What if there is nothing missing inside of you?

All forms of true healing are rooted in acceptance, accepting the totality of life, recognizing the seemingly undesirable life situations are all part of a non-dualisitc cosmic dance, part of who we are. Therefore, less-than-ness can only be created through perceived "shouldn't be's — discrepancies derived from comparing the meanings we give to "what is" versus "what I think would be favorable to my manifested forms".

*To let go of suffering and the barrier against Self-love is to let go of the need to be identified with the consequences we associate with certain events that life entails, and the reiterated past stories thereof, to let go of our egoic need for victimhood, to recognize the possibility of an expiry date to what we no longer need to re-activate in our vibrations.*

If we go beyond the illusory sense of "self" identified through past conditioning and events, and just be present — there is nothing to do, nowhere to be, no destination to get to or achieve. There is nothing to overcome to get to the other side to resume our wholeness — it is an uncaused default state of Being.

*If you listen to silence, you will hear a peaceful presence where infinite creativity lives.*

Awaken your inner potential, live in authentic Self-love, one that is rooted in inclusion rather than exclusion, inward focus rather than outward focus.

Allow connection to the profound knowingness of our infinite, all-encompassing present Being, then just learn and grow, from and be in the here and now.

\*\*\*

To contact Dr. Lau:

Website: https://drjackielaucoaching.com/
Facebook: https://www.facebook.com/drjackielaucoaching
Linkedin: https://www.linkedin.com/in/dr-jackie-lau
Email: drjackielaucoaching@gmail.com

# Joann Marchese

Joann Marchese is a seasoned Reiki Master, intuitive mindset coach, and the founder of Infinite Mindset Coaching, dedicated to helping individuals break through emotional barriers, heal from past pain, and step into the life they dreamed about. With years of experience in energy healing, subconscious reprogramming, and personal transformation, she guides clients to release self-doubt, grief, and beliefs they have outgrown so they can create lasting change.

Her passion for this work stems from her transformative journey—finding the strength to leave a toxic marriage, only to later experience the profound heartbreak of losing her second husband to cancer. Through this journey, she discovered the power of healing, self-discovery, and mindset transformation, ultimately turning her pain into purpose. Now, she helps others navigate their paths toward healing and empowerment.

As the creator of Quantum Reprogramming, Joann developed a method that uses energy work to create shifts in the mind, body, and soul. She helps individuals realign with their true selves and release what no longer serves them. She empowers clients to heal, grow, and reclaim their inner strength through a personalized approach that blends mindset coaching, energy work, and holistic techniques.

Joann believes that real transformation starts within and ripples outward, shaping our lives and the world around us. As an artist and author, she channels this belief into her books, journals, and artwork, inspiring growth, reflection, and self-empowerment.

She offers virtual and in-person coaching in Fleming Island, Florida, providing personalized guidance to help clients navigate breakthroughs and create lasting transformation.

# The Quantum Shift: Turning Pain into Power

## By Joann Marchese

I never imagined that walking away from a toxic marriage would lead me to the love of my life, only to lose him months after we said, "I do." And yet, that loss became the catalyst for something even greater profound transformation, a complete rewiring of my mind, and the birth of a process I call Quantum Reprogramming.

This journey was never just about finding love again. It was about learning to love myself first, trust the universe, and surrender to the unseen forces guiding me all along. It was about reclaiming my power, releasing the fears that had kept me trapped, and stepping into the truth that I was never meant to merely exist—I was meant to create. I came to understand that I wasn't just a passive participant in my life; I was the architect of my own reality, and by shifting my internal world, I could reshape the external one.

**Breaking the Cycle: Reclaiming My Life**

For two decades, I silenced myself, pretending that the life I was living was enough. I over-gave, abandoned my own needs, and made endless compromises, all in an attempt to keep the peace in a marriage that was slowly eroding my sense of self. I had convinced myself that love required self-sacrifice, that my worth was measured by how much I could endure. Later, I would come to realize that this was not love; it was conditioning, a belief system I had unknowingly adopted and one I would have to unlearn.

For years, I lived in survival mode, walking on eggshells to avoid conflict, suppressing my own desires, and constantly molding myself into a version of myself that felt more acceptable to others. The weight of pretending—of making myself smaller—became unbearable. I lost myself completely, convinced that this was simply how life was meant to be.

Then, something inside me shifted. My higher self—my intuition—finally broke through the noise. I realized that I hated the version of myself I had become. My soul felt drained, my body constantly sick and exhausted, as though it was physically rejecting the life I was forcing myself to live. Desperate to escape the emptiness, I sought external solutions. I underwent multiple surgeries—some completely unnecessary, believing that cutting away parts of myself could somehow heal what was broken inside. I numbed myself with medication, trying to silence the energy that kept me trapped in the same toxic cycles.

But no matter how much I altered my external reality, the truth remained: the problem wasn't outside of me—it was within. My beliefs, my programming, and my subconscious patterns were the architects of my suffering. My self-esteem had hit rock bottom, and I had endured more trauma than any one person should. I finally saw it clearly: I was no longer living but merely surviving. I was existing in an environment that my subconscious had created based on the false beliefs I had adopted about myself and what I deserved.

If I wanted to change my life, I had to start by changing myself.

That realization was my breaking point—but also my breakthrough. I could no longer ignore the truth: I had to show up for myself, uncover the roots of my pain, and finally heal in a way that was real, lasting, and entirely my own.

## The Shift Begins: Freeing My Mind and Reclaiming My Power

As I embraced the need for change, I realized that the universe had been guiding me toward Quantum Reprogramming long before I understood it. That guidance came through an intuitive pull toward energy healing—an undeniable knowing that the answers I sought lay beyond traditional methods. This pull led me to Reiki, an ancient energy healing practice that would later become a cornerstone of my work.

Studying under a Reiki Master, I not only learned the art of energy healing but was also introduced to transformative techniques like Theta Healing. This powerful modality allowed me to access and reprogram the subconscious mind in ways I had never imagined. In just three sessions, I unraveled emotional wounds that years of therapy had failed to heal. The experience was nothing short of life-changing.

Through this process, I discovered that healing wasn't just about managing pain or overcoming trauma—it was about rewiring the subconscious beliefs that shaped my reality. This realization changed everything. For the first time, I understood that the subconscious mind serves as the blueprint for our lives, influencing our perceptions, dictating our experiences, and defining what we believe we deserve. If I could shift the programming beneath the surface, I could transform my entire reality.

Looking back now, I see how the universe had been preparing me all along, leading me through experiences that revealed the profound link between belief and reality. This newfound awareness gave me the courage to break free, reclaim my power, and lay the foundation for what would later become Quantum Reprogramming.

Leaving was both terrifying and liberating. I had no idea what the future held—only that I couldn't stay where I was. With no plan but my newly reprogrammed beliefs, I stepped into the unknown, knowing that it would lead me to a better life.

That decision—choosing myself—was the first fracture in my old reality. Almost instantly, the universe responded, aligning me with my dream 12th-floor apartment overlooking downtown Pittsburgh. More than just a home, it symbolized a higher perspective, a fresh start, and proof that when we shift within, our external world follows.

For years, I had allowed others to define me, shaping my identity through their expectations and beliefs. Now, faced with a blank slate and boundless potential, I asked myself the most pivotal question: Who do I truly want to be?

The first belief I reprogrammed was I am a person of integrity. I wanted my words and actions to align—not just for others' trust, but so I could trust myself. From that moment, I committed to radical honesty—no more lies, especially to myself. That shift changed everything. Living with integrity meant making decisions that genuinely aligned with who I was and what I believed, facing mistakes with accountability, and fully accepting every aspect of myself, both inside and out, without shame. My scars became badges of armor rather than shame.

Through my journey of self-discovery, I learned to love myself in a way I never had before—to respect my own needs, honor my boundaries, and embrace my authenticity. The deeper I aligned with my truth, the more I understood that self-love was the foundation for everything, including the kind of love I would later invite into my life. This transformation was not just personal; it was preparing me for something greater.

This was my first undeniable experience of how shifting a belief could reshape my reality. It was no longer about reacting to life but rewriting it. That realization sparked my curiosity about the true potential of belief reprogramming and how far it could be pushed.

## A Love That Transformed Reality

When I met Jack, I had already begun rewriting my story, stepping into a version of myself that knew I deserved more. By embracing my power, I aligned with a love that reflected my growth—something deeper, more authentic than I had ever known. Jack entered my life at the exact moment I was ready, though I didn't yet realize our connection would shift my entire perception of reality.

Jack wasn't just my partner; he was a mirror, a teacher, and the catalyst for my greatest transformation. Our love was intense and transformative, a balance of passion, healing, challenge, and growth. It felt like a story far greater than myself—equal parts 'The Notebook' and 'Deadpool'—a connection filled with unconditional love, humor, and acceptance.

Through our relationship, I witnessed firsthand how transforming my beliefs could reshape my reality. Jack reflected back on the wounds I still needed to heal, and as I worked on reprogramming my subconscious, I saw a rapid and lasting change. This transformation allowed me to create the healthiest, most authentic relationship I had ever experienced—one where I embraced and loved even the parts of myself I once hid. It was a living testament to the power of belief, preparing me for the profound lessons that were yet to come.

Within a year, we were married. Just four and a half months later, he was gone. Stage 4 Lung Cancer surfaced suddenly, barely a month after our wedding. Exactly 365 days from the day we moved in together, he took his last breath. I know most would imagine devastation, picturing loss through their own experiences and beliefs, but my reality was something different. There was magic woven into heartbreak, a force beyond comprehension, making it clear: our story was never meant to end with grief—it was meant to awaken something far greater.

Grief has a way of distorting time, making loss feel like reality itself is shattering. When Jack took his last breath, a part of me went with him, and a new version was born. Jack's love didn't leave me when he passed—it expanded. It propelled me forward, fueling my healing and inspiring me to create the best life possible for both of us. His love gave me the strength to consciously choose beliefs that supported my healing rather than kept me in pain. Even when others expected me to remain in mourning, I knew Jack wouldn't want that for me. He would have wanted me to take everything I had learned and use it to build something meaningful. That belief fueled me, transforming my grief into purpose and allowing me to help others reclaim control over their lives.

## The Birth of Quantum Reprogramming

The day after he passed—exactly one year from when I moved in with him—I had a vision. A cosmic symmetry. He appeared to me, his presence undeniable.

"You did it," he said.

In that instant, something within me shifted. I realized that I wasn't just grieving the loss of my husband; I was stepping into something far greater. I could feel the last traces of my need for external validation dissolved. Suddenly, the things I had once cared about—money, appearance, societal expectations—no longer held any weight. Instead, I was filled with overwhelming peace, something I had never felt before. It was as though I had been released from fear itself, yet that absence was so unfamiliar and profound that it was initially overwhelming.

As I witnessed Jack's passing affect those around me in profoundly different ways, I realized that each person was experiencing grief through the lens of their own wounds, fears, and beliefs. This realization became the catalyst for what would evolve into Quantum Reprogramming. Healing wasn't just about working through grief or overcoming past pain; it was about consciously reshaping the subconscious beliefs that define our experiences.

In the months that followed, I began receiving undeniable insights into how the mind shapes reality. I was guided to explore concepts I had never previously considered in a wide range of subjects — religion, mysticism, science, quantum theory, space, history, and alternative healing. I immersed myself in books, articles, and hours of research, diving deep into the knowledge that felt as though it had been waiting for me all along. It felt as though the universe had enveloped me in a cocoon, removing distractions so I could fully absorb the wisdom that would ultimately shape Quantum Reprogramming.

I confirmed that beliefs don't just shape reality—they create it. The subconscious mind acts as an internal operating system, influencing perception, reactions, and the opportunities we allow ourselves. By reprogramming my subconscious, I found I could transform my life—aligning with purpose, abundance, and clarity.

I began recognizing patterns I had once overlooked — how thoughts, emotions, and beliefs serve as blueprints for our experiences. The more I explored, the clearer it became: our external world is a reflection of our internal programming.

I tested this understanding repeatedly, and each time, I saw the same result—whenever I reprogrammed the way I perceived reality, my external world responded.

My entire reality shifted as I dismantled limiting beliefs and replaced them with empowering truths. What began as a personal transformation evolved into Quantum Reprogramming—a process designed to help others break free from outdated subconscious patterns and create the life they truly desire. I combined everything I had learned into a holistic approach, blending energy work, subconscious reprogramming, and profound self-discovery to rewire the subconscious mind to break old cycles and step into a reality of empowerment and expansion.

Quantum Reprogramming is about identifying and transforming deep-seated subconscious beliefs at the energetic level. It integrates science, energy work, and mindset coaching to create real, lasting change. It is a customized, systematic approach to reshaping the subconscious mind, collapsing outdated mental patterns, breaking ancestral cycles, and stepping into an entirely new reality. This process helps heal deep emotional wounds, including trauma, grief, anxiety, and depression, by addressing the root subconscious beliefs that keep people stuck in suffering. By identifying and shifting these limiting beliefs, individuals can break free from the cycles that have unconsciously shaped their lives and create a new, empowered reality.

This is more than simple mindset work. More than affirmations. It is like upgrading a computer's operating system—except this time, the computer is your mind. Most people are still running on the same subconscious programming they developed by age seven, operating on autopilot with outdated belief systems they have long outgrown. Imagine trying to run your business today on the same computer you used when you were seven years old. You wouldn't—you would upgrade it. So why wouldn't you invest in upgrading the most powerful personal computer you own—your mind?

To amplify the transformation, I incorporated Reiki, an ancient Japanese energy healing technique, into the process. Reiki works by channeling universal life force energy to promote physical, emotional, and spiritual healing. I realized that while the subconscious mind was being reprogrammed, the body also needed to heal. Reiki allows the body to release stored trauma and energetic blockages, creating space for the subconscious shifts to take hold. Healing on all levels—mind, body, and energy—accelerated the transformation process.

Together, Quantum Reprogramming and Reiki help identify the core beliefs that shape thought patterns, behaviors, and emotional triggers. Once these beliefs are brought to the surface, they are rewired into new patterns that are more self-serving and aligned with one's highest potential. This process isn't about bypassing pain but transforming it into wisdom and empowerment.

I saw the proof in my own life. Quantum Reprogramming allowed me to not only heal after Jack passed but also to create a belief system that empowered me to live my best life. Through this process, I was able to open myself to a new love story—one that feels like a continuation of the first, filled with love, acceptance, and magic. The more I reprogrammed, the more miraculous shifts unfolded before me. This entire journey led me to one undeniable truth: the more you free your mind, the more you elevate your life. By shifting our internal world, we unlock a completely different external reality filled with infinite possibilities.

## The Ripple Effect: Changing the World One Mind at a Time

Jack may have physically left this world, but his love never left me. Instead, it became the catalyst that awakened me to my true purpose, igniting a mission far greater than I ever imagined. He will always be my reason why. His presence, even beyond the physical, continues to guide me, reminding me that transformation is possible for anyone willing to take the leap.

My vision is clear: I am here to share Quantum Reprogramming with the world, to help others break free from the subconscious limitations that keep them trapped in cycles of fear, doubt, and suffering. I envision a world where people awaken to their power, no longer seeing themselves as victims of circumstance but as conscious creators of their reality—a world where we operate from alignment, truth, and infinite possibility rather than fear and restriction.

We are on the brink of a global shift—one that starts with the individual. Imagine a world where healing, self-love, and empowerment are the norm rather than suffering and limitation. Imagine generations raised without inherited fears, without deeply ingrained beliefs that tell them they are not enough. Imagine a world where people instinctively understand the power of their thoughts, emotions, and ability to shape their own lives.

This work is bigger than me — bigger than any one person. It is a movement, a revolution of the mind that starts within each of us. Healing is not just a personal journey; it is a collective one. As we heal ourselves, we heal the world. Every belief we shift, every fear we dissolve, and every limitation we release creates a ripple effect that extends far beyond what we can see.

Looking back, I now see that every moment—every heartbreak, loss, challenge—was a steppingstone guiding me to this realization. Each experience was an initiation into deeper wisdom, proof that we are all capable of rewriting our reality. We are all capable of stepping into the highest, most empowered version of ourselves.

The only question is: Are you ready to break free?

***

**Let's Connect:**

Joann Marchese

Infinite Mindset I Phone: 904.657.0555

Website: https://infinitemindsetcoaching.org/
Email: info@infinitemindsetcoaching.org
Linktree: https://linktr.ee/infinitemindsetcoaching
Socials: @infinitemindsetcoaching (Instagram, TikTok, Facebook, and You Tube)

✨ **Free Your Mind - Elevate Your Life.** ✨

# Afterword

Life is always a series of transitions... people, places and things that shape who we are as individuals. Often, you never know that the next catalyst for change is around the corner.

Jim Britt and Jim Lutes have spent decades influencing individuals to blossom into the best version of themselves.

Allow all you have read in this book to create introspection and redirection if required. It's your journey to craft.

*The Change* is a series. A global movement. Watch for future releases and add them to your collection. If you know of anyone who would like to be considered as a co-author for a future book, have them email our offices at support@jimbritt.com.

The individual and combined works of Jim Britt and Jim Lutes have filled seminar rooms to maximum capacity and created a worldwide demand.

The blessings go both ways as Jim and Jim are always willing students of life. Out of demand for life-changing programs and events, Jim and Jim conduct seminars worldwide.

To Schedule Jim Britt or Jim Lutes as your featured speaker at your next convention or special event, email Jim Britt at: support@jimbritt.com or Jim Lutes at: mindpowerpro@yahoo.com

For more info on Jim & Jim visit: www.LutesInternational.com or www.JimBritt.com

Master your moment as they become hours that become days.

Do something remarkable today! Your legacy awaits.

Blessings,

Jim Britt and Jim Lutes

www.ingramcontent.com/pod-product-compliance
Lightning Source LLC
LaVergne TN
LVHW021808060526
838201LV00058B/3286